645 M26 C

5/75

The Complete Book of CURTAINS, SLIPCOVERS & UPHOLSTERY

The Complete Book of
CURTAINS,
SLIPCOVERS &
UPHOLSTERY

Marguerite Maddox and
Miriam Morrison Peake

Gramercy Publishing Company
New York

This edition is published by Gramercy Publishing Company,
a division of Crown Publishers, Inc.
by arrangement with Simon & Schuster, Inc.
abcdefgh
Manufactured in the United States of America.

c   d   e   f   g   h

Acknowledgments

THE AUTHORS are deeply indebted to the following experts who have so generously contributed of their time and technical knowledge in the preparation of this book: The Educational Bureau of Coats & Clark Inc., 430 Park Avenue, New York City; Mrs. Dennie H. Carter, stylist, Consolidated Trimming Corporation, 27 West 23rd Street, New York City; Mr. Arthur W. Evers, Kirsch Company, 2 Prospect Street, Sturgis, Michigan; and Mrs. Mae Weston, fashion consultant, Bates Fabrics, Inc., 112 West 34th Street, New York City.

They are further indebted to their friends Miss Isabelle Vaughan and Mrs. Nell Clairmonte, of New York City, the artists who so skillfully interpreted their ideas in these illustrations.

Contents

Draperies (continued)

Bedspreads 175

Dressing Tables 211

How to Use This Book

EVERYONE has some decorating problem, from a tired chair to the complete rejuvenation of an entire room. This often seems like a major financial outlay, but it need not be so. You will find that by saving labor costs these problems can be solved within your budget. Some of these projects may be done by hand; others require the use of a sewing machine—if you do not have one, do you know that they can be rented for only a few dollars a week?

While writing this book, we have checked our methods by making draperies, slipcovers and bedspreads. And you should see how many swags we now have at our windows! We hope these pages will not only fill your immediate needs, but will also open up a whole field of new adventures. Before starting out on your decorating journey, plan your destination by using this book as a road map.

Leaf through the pages to find the answers to your particular problem. Then, when your first project has been completed and shows you how much can be accomplished, you will want to start planning for your next major goal. Little side trips into the bypaths of decorating can also be great fun.

Points of information in each section may well come in handy for another section: for example, the method of making scallops applies equally to bedspreads, café curtains or valances. There are innumerable guideposts to help you along your way; use the index to find them.

After you have decided on colors, fabrics and measurements for a particular purpose, read through the pertinent instructions to see what supplies you will need. Make a complete shopping list so that you will have all the equipment on hand before you start work. Different jobs require different supplies. A shopping list for draperies, for example, will include such things as rods, lining, stiffening, drapery hooks, rings, cords or shirring tape, matching thread, needles, pins and weights. On the other hand, a shopping list for slipcovers will include welting, zippers, heavy-duty thread and pins that are longer than dressmaker pins. All of these will be found in most department stores, fabric shops and many of them in variety and hardware stores.

Charts for approximate yardages, threads and needle sizes and zippers are included.

The Complete Book of CURTAINS, SLIPCOVERS & UPHOLSTERY

The Art of Color

ALMOST every woman knows exactly what
flowers she likes, what colors she responds to.
Most people have strong color preferences but do
not always know how to blend these colors into a
beautiful symphony which satisfies and charms the be-
holder. But this is not an impossible art. A little ex-
perimentation with fabrics, wall paints and papers,
a focusing on a prized single object in a room—a painting, portrait, a treasured vase or other *objet d'art*—
the adjusting to new and untried color combinations
and the results will be as rewarding in the new bloom-
ing of your home as the quiet, restful pleasure one
obtains from making a perfect arrangement of ex-
quisite springtime flowers.

For your convenience we have designed and printed
a "color wheel" on the back cover of this volume. The
"wheel" is constructed of spools of thread. When planning a color scheme for any room we have always
found it helpful to gather up a handful of spools of
thread we fancy at a notion counter. These, and an as-
sortment of paint "chips" (small sample paint cards)
from your local paint dealer are invaluable to have in
hand when you go to shop for your fabrics. The matching of color or the skillful blending of the various

1

shades and tones comes from practice unless one is blessed with true color "memory."

THE THREE CLASSES OF COLOR

There are three classes: Primary, Secondary, Tertiary.

The Primary Colors are: Red, Yellow, Blue. All other colors are a mixture of these three.

The Secondary Colors are: Orange, Green and Purple. These are made from the following combinations: orange is red plus yellow; green is yellow plus blue; purple is red plus blue.

The Tertiary or Neutralized Colors are produced by mixing any color and its opposite or near opposite, providing the proportions are right. Incidentally, the greatest beauty is inherent in these *grayed* colors as their effect on body skin-tones is much kinder than the pure, strong colors.

The Warm Colors are: Red, Yellow, Orange, with orange being the warmest of the colors.

The Cool Colors are: Blue, Green, Violet, with blue being the coolest of the colors.

Black, White and Gray are *neutral* colors.

Warm colors are "advancing" (seem to come toward one), enlarging and stimulating in effect. The eye focuses on red, for instance, in such a way that the warm color dress or fabric seems nearer to the eye than it actually is.

Cool colors are receding in effect—they seem to diminish or make the object look farther away and smaller. Cool colors have long been known to have a quieting effect on the mind and the emotions.

THE TERMINOLOGY OF COLOR

Hue is color identification: blue, green, yellow, red, etc.

Value is the range of a single color: light, medium, dark and very dark.

Chroma is the color strength: pure red, for example, is saturated or high in red intensity; pink is lower in red intensity or chroma.

Tint is pure color lightened with white—pastels are tints.

Shade is pure color darkened with black or deep value, as in midnight blue.

COLOR HARMONY

In assembling and coordinating the colors in a room, color harmony is achieved by any one of these methods:

1. *Blending of Colors:* Every color shares one common color base, such as a blue-green, green and a yellow-green. Using a dark blue, let us say, as a basic color foundation, add blue-green or green in other fabrics in the room. Now add accessory color such as violet or blue-violet. This system is effective and produces a most attractive over-all decorative scheme. The color ranges of pinks, greens, yellows—all the various shades and hues, any "blend" of colors which have the same *base* can be manipulated in this way to your pleasure and satisfaction.

2. *A Monochromatic Color Scheme:* One in which a self-harmony of colors is used. This means using the *same color* with variations due to light or dark tints or shades in the color. Again using our dark blue merely as an example of basic color, have the accessories, trimmings or various furniture pieces slipcovered in a pastel blue or a Della Robbia blue or a soft grey-blue to produce a monochromatic effect.

3. *Color Contrast:* The color directly across from any chosen color on a color "wheel" is its opposite (see the color wheel on the back cover): blue is contrasted by orange; red by green; the secondary color, violet, is directly opposite yellow. Returning again to our example of blue, it would make a sharp *contrast* if we chose red, yellow, red-orange or yellow-orange in our decorating scheme.

With a little thoughtful study you can become expert in the art of boldly contrasting or delicately blending colors for the decorating of your home interiors. Try experimenting with scraps of colored cottons, silks, wool yarns. Test lengths of fabric by placing them side by side as smart interior decorators do.

The decorating rules for choosing colors and fabrics for your slipcovering, drapery making, upholstering are really quite simple: Use only *one* patterned fabric in a room and this preferably in the drapery or slipcover fabric. Striped materials may also be used together with a patterned fabric such as a flower print, a scenic print, but have the colors of the stripes complementary to the colors of the patterned material. Color-scheme the entire room from the patterned design (if you are using one) by taking the other colors, either blended or monochromatic, from the ones of the most prominent fabric in your room. Do not use more than three or four colors in any one room. Use basic, neutral, but cheerful colors for the backgrounds. Large pieces of overstuffed furniture, such as big davenports or Chesterfields, should be "faded" into your wall colors by using fabric which does not stand out too prominently and thus "jump" a large piece of furniture into the room. It makes for an unbalanced look not to have the furniture well blended into the over-all aspect. Also the best decision regarding the use of bright colors as accents or accessories is *always* to use these bright spots in small amounts.

Happily, there is no color which is out of date and no color which is "not being used this year." Color is a highly personal thing. If you like it, are happy with your preferred color range, by all means stick to it. Just don't let it overwhelm you! If you like warm colors, use them, remembering that these are most successful in a northern exposure. Cool colors, such as blue or green, are most successful in rooms with a southern exposure, but let your preference be your guide. *Blend* your colors and you will be happier with them than if you try to "match up" everything. This is a difficult thing to do as there are literally thousands of variations, and who wants everything "matched" anyway?

Fabrics

THE RUG or the carpeting is usually the determining factor in choosing the fabrics and colors for your draperies. If you have good Oriental rugs, the window treatments should be in a plain color; if wall-to-wall carpeting in a solid color graces your floors, then by all means use a handsomely figured fabric for your draperies. Many decorators also choose fabrics to correlate with a good painting, a favorite collection of china, needlepoint chairs or other various prized heirlooms or possessions.

We mention only a few of literally thousands of designs and weaves of fabrics to choose from at your drapery shop, department stores, mill-end shops, and from decorators who will show you samples of the finest fabrics made in this country and in Europe. These decorator fabrics, beautiful but expensive, can be ordered only by a decorator for you. In this case the professional decorator makes a profit on the transaction but no more than a department store does. The customer pays the retail price; the decorator has the value of the professional discount from the fabric manufacturer. If you are spending a large sum for fabrics, ordering through a qualified decorator is indeed a boon to you.

6

FABRICS FOR FORMAL USE

Brocade (Silk): A heavy raised design woven on a plain background; design is in color and has a slightly padded feeling.

Damask (Silk): Silk with a woven satin design raised on a dull-textured background. One of the most useful and satisfying of all drapery fabrics because it hangs in soft graceful folds.

Faille (Silk): Silk with a horizontal ribbing; it may be of all silk or silk and synthetic threads. The pure silk variety is very soft and flexible; the synthetics have more body and are quite a bit stiffer. The heavier types are used for upholstering French- and English-type chairs and sofas; in boldly ribbed synthetics, heavy failles are a good choice for modern furniture styles.

Linens and Linens with Rayon: Good linens are in a higher priced range than cottons and *Crewel Embroidered Linens* are expensive but are completely handsome and wear exceedingly well for years and years.

Moire (Silk): This has a faille background pressed down to make a wavy, irregular pattern, which we used to know as "watered silk," and is used mostly with traditional eighteenth-century furniture and rooms, but it is also handsome with good modern decors.

Modern De Luxe Fabrics: Many have gold threads, tarnish-proof metal foil, cellophane, grass or straw fibers woven into them, producing rich "nubbly" effects in materials ranging from silks, satins, rayons, to lightweight and heavy wools.

Reproductions: These are reproductions of eighteenth-century fabrics used at famous Williamsburg in Virginia; they are in chintz, satins, taffetas and are not as expensive as one would expect. They are most suitable for traditional rooms and furniture.

Satin: The pure silk satins have largely been replaced today by cotton-backed satins or the very satisfactory rayon mixtures, which are moderately priced; for formal use these fabrics drape beautifully.

Taffeta (Silk): These are made of real silk or mixed with synthetic fibers. A plain color taffeta has just one color; changeable taffeta is woven in two colors, one in the weft and the other in the warp, so that a changing color effect is obtained in different lights—sunlight or artificial light. A silk taffeta absorbs more light than does a satin fabric and does not reflect light in the striking way satin does. Pure silk taffeta, however, is a real luxury inasmuch as sunlight does, in time, crack it thus causing a short life. But where a note of luxury is needed, taffeta sofa pillows are wonderfully decorative and eye-pleasing.

Toile de Jouy: Often referred to simply as "toile" (pronounced "twal"), it is a fine quality chintz printed by copper roller process; the pattern is usually all one color printed on a plain background. Beautiful scenic designs are found in the toiles; the fabric is splendid for draperies, bedspreads, screens and pillows.

Velvet: This fabric may be cotton-backed, has a high woven "pile" and may be a synthetic weave and thus in the inexpensive price range. It is widely used as chair seat covering and as decorative pillow material.

FABRICS FOR SEMIFORMAL USE

Antique Satin: Backed with cotton, this medium-priced material has excellent wearing qualities, drapes well, dry cleans well, comes in an almost inexhaustible range of colors.

Acetate Rayon Taffeta: Also known as Celanese taffetas, these are much less expensive than silk taffetas, come in many colors, drape well at windows but do not have the intriguing crispness of a pure silk fabric—however, this is a fabric much in demand in all parts of the country.

Barkcloth: An all-cotton fabric in both solid colors and prints; has a smooth texture and is used mostly for slipcovers and draperies.

Chintzes: They are made of cotton, have an even weave that takes color well, are lightweight. When shopping for chintzes you will find these desirable materials in unglazed finish, in semiglazed and the highly glazed—the latter being the most expensive and also the most satisfactory as it has a high-gloss permanent finish.

Corduroy: This is a pile fabric woven so as to make vertical ridges; either coarse ridges or narrow and fine. The dressier types may be used on chairs or sofas in place of the more expensive velvets. The small-ridge or "small-wale" type comes in a wide range of colors from light to very dark and is favored over the wide-wale type found in only a narrow color range.

Printed Fabrics: Cretonnes, linens, chintzes are included in this category. The design and price range runs from decidedly inexpensive roller printed materials to the better merchandise, which is beautifully printed by the hand-block technique.

Printed Fiberglas: Having the advantage of being fully fireproof, these are increasingly obtainable in good modern designs. They are especially attractive in contemporary houses with wide picture windows or partially glassed-in walls. Fiberglas should be used only for draperies or curtains—*never* as a slipcover material.

FABRICS FOR INFORMAL USE

Awning Cloth—Striped: An extremely durable, heavy cotton, particularly attractive in gay stripes, it is used for slipcovers on porch and patio chairs and chaises.

Cotton Broadcloth: One of the most satisfactory and inexpensive materials ever devised, it has a soft drape, comes in a variety of colors. Use it for draperies, slipcovers, bedspreads.

Chambray: This is simply a soft cotton gingham-like fabric without the variegated color of a gingham. It has a good body and is suitable for draperies and bedspreads when economy is a prime consideration.

Cottons—Polished: There is a tremendous vogue for polished cottons in plain colors and in magnificent color prints. Many of the latter are imported; the price range is medium to slightly expensive, but no more desirable fabric is to be found in the market. Perfect for draperies, bedspreads, slipcovers.

Cotton Repp: An economy fabric, but apt to fade in a short time so it should be considered as a temporary measure and if possible kept where it is not subjected to strong sunlight when used for draperies or as slip-covers.

Duck: A heavy, inexpensive cotton that has a long life; a multitude of uses in rooms that get hard use; on patios, porches, in dens.

Denim: This fabric has been enormously smartened up by designers; it is sturdy, good-looking and not high in cost.

Gingham: Made of cotton; found in bright colors, muted colors, a most useful fabric for informal effects.

Indianhead: A closely woven cotton with a smooth finish. The name is simply a trade name and known to every home sewer and home decorator. Use it for cheerful, crisp-looking cafe curtains, in cottage-type living rooms, for bedspreads—a myriad of simple, unaffected uses.

Monk's Cloth: Another inexpensive, loosely woven cotton, which is popular for college rooms, for the first one-room apartment of career girls, for dens, playrooms.

Sail Cloth: Woven of cotton so there is no top or bottom, right side or wrong side, this handy material may be used lengthwise, crosswise, any way you like! It is a fairly heavy but easy-to-handle fabric available in a wide range of colors and prints; especially used for slipcovers or draperies where a minimum amount of care is desirable.

Sateen: A fine cotton in a satin-smooth weave; can be used for draperies, slipcovers, bedspreads, dressing tables. Pretty and to be found in a veritable rainbow range of colors in various qualities and at different prices. The cheaper varieties are the accepted fabric for lining draperies.

Ticking: Just what the term implies—mattress ticking—but so good-looking these days that it is favored by smart decorators even in extremely chic apartments and houses. Easy to handle for slipcovers, draperies. The colors are luscious!

Unbleached Muslin: A very inexpensive cotton cloth that serves as bedspreads and draperies for temporary use until one can spend more money for permanent acquisition in fabrics.

Slipcovers

THERE ARE hundreds of different kinds of chairs—armchairs, straight chairs, overstuffed chairs and chairs with wooden frames, delicate French chairs, imposing Italian and Spanish chairs, modern chairs—too many to list and certainly too many to illustrate here. However, we have chosen the types that show most of the features you may encounter in making a slipcover. Among them we believe you will find a back, an arm, a cushion, that will have some resemblance to the chair you wish to transform. The instructions can be adapted to almost any shape.

Overstuffed Chairs

Fig. 1   Boudoir chair with cushion
Fig. 2   Chair with square back and arms
Fig. 3   Lounge chair with cushion
Fig. 4   Easy chair with cushion
Fig. 5   Victorian chair with scroll back and arms, T-cushion
Fig. 6   Wing chair
Fig. 7   Armchair with barrel back
Fig. 8   Lounge chair with semidetached back cushion
Fig. 9   Channel-back chair with no cushion
Fig. 10 Barrel-back chair with T-cushion

13

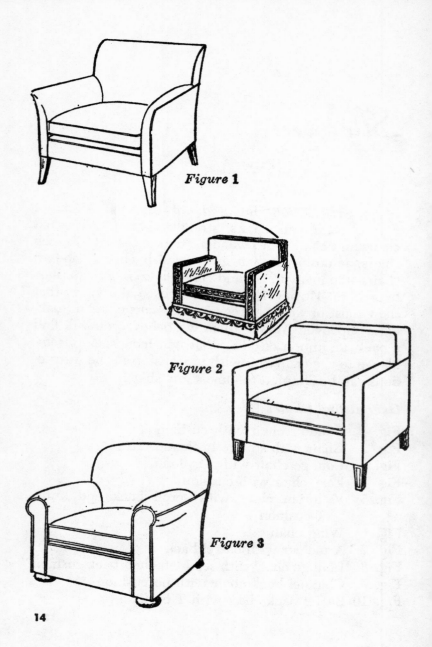

Figure 1

Figure 2

Figure 3

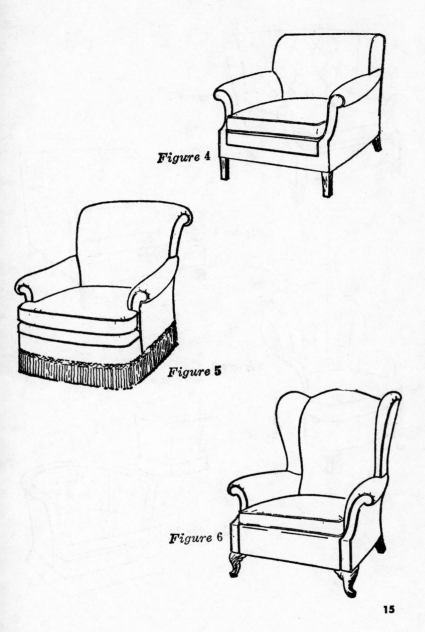

Figure 4

Figure 5

Figure 6

Figure 7

Figure 8

Figure 9

Figure 10

16

Chairs with Wooden Frames

Fig. 11   Armchair with open back and arms, no cushion

Fig. 12   French armchair with closed back and arms, cushion

Fig. 13   Victorian chair with closed semi-arms and closed back

Fig. 14   Side chair with open back and padded arms

Fig. 15   Channel-back armchair, closed back, open arms

Fig. 16   Slipper chair

Sofas

Fig. 17   Two-cushion love seat

Fig. 18   Modern two-seat sofa with semidetached back cushions

Fig. 19   Modern three-seat sofa, semidetached back cushions

Fig. 20   Traditional three-cushion sofa

Fig. 21   Three-cushion sofa with curved back and arms

Fig. 22   Victorian sofa, no cushion

Fig. 23   Chaise

Fig. 24   Three-seat sofa

MATERIALS

Fabrics: Many various kinds of fabrics suitable for slipcovers are described on pages 7–12. Find the type of chair or sofa that most closely resembles yours at the beginning of this section, then see the yardage chart on page 112. If you plan to use self-welting (cording

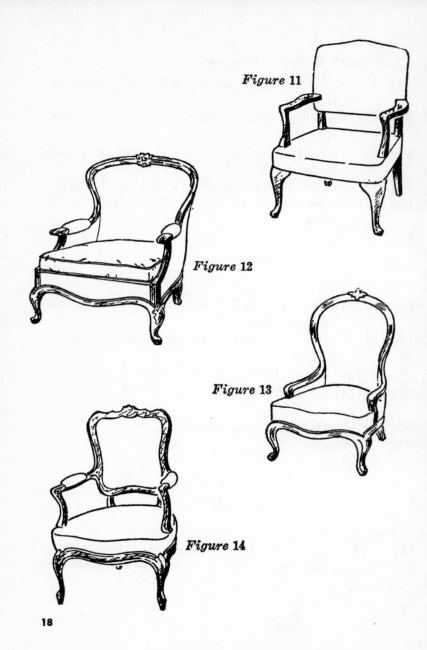

Figure 11

Figure 12

Figure 13

Figure 14

Figure 15

Figure 16

Figure 17

Figure 18

Figure 19

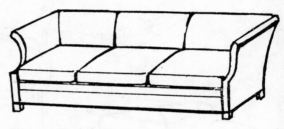

Figure 20

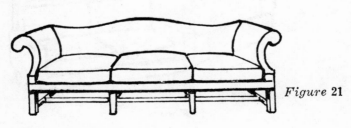

Figure 21

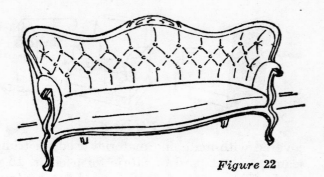

Figure 22

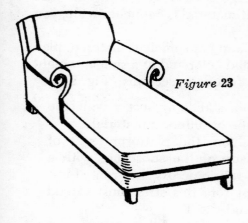

Figure 23

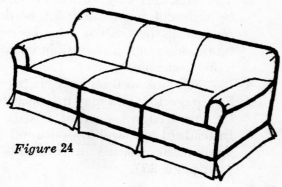

Figure 24

Figure 25

covered with matching material used for trimming the seams), add 1 yard of fabric for a chair, 1½ yards for a sofa. This extra yardage is used for cutting the bias strips for the welting. If material is 54 inches wide, you may need slightly less.

Should you be unable to get sufficient material, plan to use a substitute of solid color and of a similar weight for one or more of the following sections (Fig. 25):

1. If the chair or sofa stands against a wall, the outside back can be of different material.

2. If there is a cushion, the platform (seat of chair) can be made of the substitute with a strip of the main fabric across the front; for a T-cushion chair or sofa this strip must extend a few inches behind the T.

3. The back and side borders of the cushions can be different from the front borders; also the reverse of the cushion may be made of other fabric, although a reversible cushion is always more desirable.

4. If it will look well on your chair (see chair No. 5 on page 15), you may use deep fringe around the lower edge instead of a skirt.

5. Instead of self-welting, use other trimming, ready-made welting or reverse French seams (see page 26).

6. In some informal rooms one may see slipcovers made of two different materials—body of one fabric and ruffled skirt, cushion and welting of another. Both these fabrics should then be repeated in other parts of the room, and unless very carefully balanced and well planned the result may be rather jumbled in appearance. If you wish to use two materials, test the actual fabric on the various pieces of furniture to achieve proper color balance before you put shears to fabric.

Lining Material: The skirt of a slipcover should be lined to avoid a hemline mark and to give proper body to the skirt. For this, you may use any soft white or unbleached material, such as an old sheet or about 2 yards of sateen, muslin or similar inexpensive fabric.

Welting: This is corded trimming for seams. Most often it is cord covered with the same fabric as the slipcover and is called "self-welting." Instructions for making this will be given later. About 18 yards of welting are necessary for a chair, 36 yards for a sofa. Ready-made welting can also be bought in a variety of colors. The color and texture must blend with the slipcover fabric or repeat another color used in the same room. Do not put cotton-covered welting on a satin slipcover; if you prefer a contrast, such as white on a blue cover, or want to accent one of the colors in the pattern, it is better to buy a yard or more of this color in a fabric of similar weight and finish as the slipcover, and then use this to make your own welting. This is a better procedure than to use ready-made welting that does not harmonize with the slipcover.

Figure 26

Figure 27

Figure 28

Figure 29

Figure 30

Figure 31

Figure 32

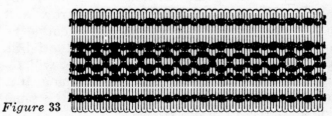

Figure 33

Trimmings: Trimmings of various kinds are available in most upholstery departments; see Figs. 26–33 for some of the many different types. One of the most popular of these is moss fringe, which comes in many colors of both cotton and rayon. Again, the particular fringe must be suitable for the slipcover. Moss fringe often provides a good contrast on solid colors. Decorative braid is also often used to outline borders and cushion (see Fig. 2 on page 14).

Deep fringe makes an excellent skirt on certain types of furniture, particularly in a Victorian setting. Select a fringe that will go well with the slipcover fabric in texture and color, making certain that it is the right length to reach from the base of the front border to within 1 or 2 inches of the floor (see Fig. 5 on page 15).

Reverse French Seams: These can be used instead of welting or trimming. To make these, first pin, cut and notch the slipcover sections as directed in a later part of this section. When sewing the seams, stitch about ¼ inch outside the seam lines. When the seam is completed, trim away seam allowance so that it measures about ⅜ inch. Turn seam right side out (Fig. 34) and crease the seam on the stitching line. Pin the crease to keep the stitching line even along the edge of the fold. Now stitch again, this time ¼ inch inside the previous line of stitching. This forms a narrow welt on the right side. When sewing around a curve, be sure to ease in the fullness evenly to keep the fabric from pulling or slanting on either side; this will require basting around the curves before stitching. It is also important to keep these seams exactly the same width on all parts of the slipcover.

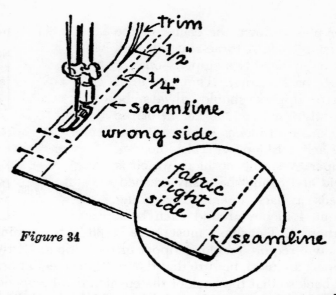

Figure 34

Zippers: These may be used on any opening that remains closed at one end, such as those on slipcovers for overstuffed chairs and sofas, or for those where the arms are all in one piece with the back or seat. When there is a space between back and seat, or when the arm is "open" with a space underneath it, the slipcover will have to open completely so that the sections can be removed. For this type of open back or open arm, use jacket zippers or snap fastener tape.

On a chair, the one-piece slipcover usually opens along one edge of the outside back. The fan-back or butterfly chair must have an opening provided down the center back. Select a zipper that is 2 or 3 inches shorter than the length from the top of the back to the floor. Zipper chart will be found on page 244.

One-piece slipcovers for sofas may have one or two closings; a two-seat sofa usually needs only one zipper placed down the center of the outside back. A three-seat sofa will probably need two zippers—one for each back corner. The length of these zippers should always be slightly less than the height of the back; 2 to 3 inches less is safest.

Each cushion will also need a zipper. A spring cushion, which is rigid and cannot be easily crushed, needs a back opening extending about 4 inches around each back

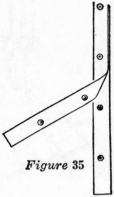

Figure 35

corner. A T-cushion must have a 36-inch opening; this will require one long zipper or two zippers. If two zippers are used, be sure that the pull-tabs meet at center back so that the back of the cushion can be opened all the way. Foam rubber or down cushions, which are soft and flexible, need only to open across the back, to within an inch or so of the back corners.

Snap Fastener Tape: This can be bought by the yard (Fig. 35). Since this will open along its entire length, it is used for closings on the slipcovers intended for chairs or sofas with open backs and arms. Here the slipcover needs an opening on each side of the back and behind the front posts of each arm. Snap tape can also be used for the separate arm covers on padded open arms (see Fig. 14 on page 18), or for any similar pieces that must open up completely for removal. Directions for sewing on snap fastener tape will be given later.

Cording Foot for Sewing Machine: When welting is used, a cording foot is required. The needle should be at the *left* of the cording foot so that the raw edges of seams will be at right, under the machine, and the bulk of the fabric can remain on the left. Use a heavy machine needle, about size 14 to 18 (see needle chart on page 243), and adjust the stitch to about 12 per inch. The tension should be loose enough so that fabric will not pull. When sewing around a corner, where the seam allowance must be clipped to keep it from pulling, stitch twice over this section of the seam to avoid ripping; break the thread, go back and start sewing again over the previous line of stitching.

Other Accessories:

Thread: About four to six spools of heavy duty thread to match fabric.

Pins: You will need a box of pins, preferably 1¼ inches long. Discard any blunt, bent or broken pins. If fabric is delicate or light in color, use only new, clean pins.

Chalk or Colored Pencil: This is for marking seam lines and must be in a color that will show clearly against the wrong side of the fabric.

Shears: They should be sharp and large enough to cut cleanly.

Yardstick: This is a necessity for marking off bias strips for use in covering welting. It is also a guide for keeping fabric straight up and down on vertical sections of the furniture and for marking the position of seams on the arms of overstuffed chairs and sofas.

Ruler: The yardstick will not always fit under the overhang of back and arms, so a ruler is needed for measuring the depth of skirt around the lower edge of the chair, as well as for measuring the depth of tuck-in.

Tape Measure or Steel Tape: This is for measuring sections of furniture when planning yardages of fabric or trimming.

Small Table: When sewing large sections of slipcover together, place the table to the left or behind the sewing machine where it can support the weight of the fabric and keep it from sliding. A larger table, such as a bridge table, will serve for cutting the skirt, cushion sections and bias strips.

SLIPCOVERS FOR OVERSTUFFED CHAIRS

These are chairs that have no visible wooden frames; only the legs are free of upholstery.

Preparation

Examine the types of chairs shown on pages 14–19. Select the one that most closely resembles the one you wish to slipcover. These pictures show the seams of the upholstery; check them against the seams on your chair. These seams must be followed as closely as possible when making the slipcover. However, there are a few seams on a slipcover that must be determined before starting work.

Remove any cushion and bring the chair out into the center of the floor to give yourself plenty of working space. Fig. 36 shows the different parts of a chair and identifies them by name.

Decide where the top of the skirt is to be. The usual length of the skirt is about 8 inches above the floor. A

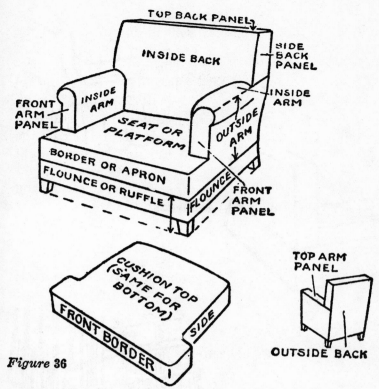

Figure 36

ruffled skirt or box-pleated skirt may start farther up, even at the edge of the platform or seat, although this is not recommended because the slipcover will not stay firmly anchored. Another look at the pictures of different chairs may help you to decide which type and length of skirt will look best on your chair. There are several types of skirts that can be made for slipcovers, but only a few of these are recommended for home sewing:

Ruffled Skirt (Fig. 37): This is simple to make, but takes a great deal more material than a tailored skirt. It

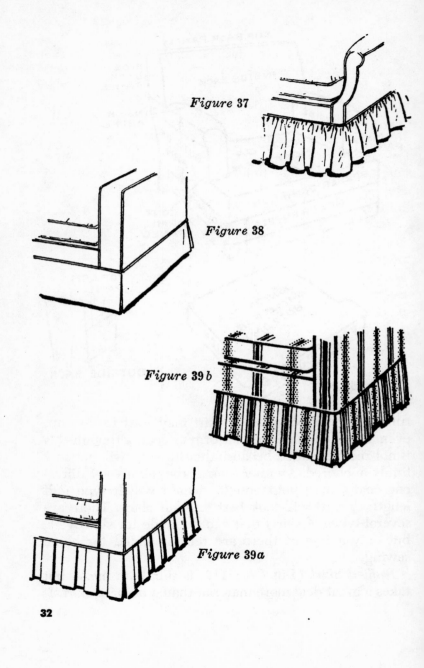

Figure 37

Figure 38

Figure 39 b

Figure 39 a

32

is suitable only for very informal settings, such as Early American furniture or bedrooms.

Kick Pleats (Fig. 38): This is a very simple skirt to make and requires the least amount of material. It looks well in any setting and on any type of furniture; it is favored by professional decorators.

Simulated Kick Pleats: Each section is made separately, lined and hemmed. Edges of sections meet at corners, and the openings between them are concealed by flaps.

Box Pleats (Figs. 39 a and 39 b): This type of skirt is not recommended because it takes a great deal of material, is difficult to plan so that the pleats fit exactly on all four sides, and because the many thicknesses are apt to break the needle on a home sewing machine.

Knife Pleats (Fig. 40): These are similar to box pleats except that they all fall in the same direction on each side of the chair.

Multiple Kick Pleats (Fig. 41): This is a group of two or three overlapping pleats forming each side of the kick pleats. They are very handsome, but the overlapping pleats may create too many thicknesses for the average home sewing machine. If the fabric is light in weight, however, you may want to try them; they can be easily converted into regular kick pleats should the machine refuse to sew through the extra thickness.

Swags and Jabots (Fig. 42): On certain types of furniture these can be most effective in the proper setting. The chair will need a plain skirt underneath the swags to hide the legs and the space under the chair.

33

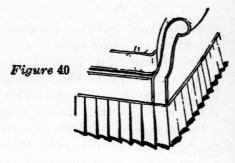

Figure 40

Figure 41

Figure 42

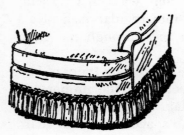

Figure 43

34

Instructions for making decorative swags and jabots will be found on pages 151–165.

Fringe (Fig. 43): Deep fringe can be used instead of a skirt, provided it is suitable for the type of chair and the other decorations in the room. When used in the proper setting, it is most attractive and by far the easiest way to finish a slipcover.

When you have chosen the type of skirt you wish to make and have decided on the length, find the distance from the floor for top of skirt at front of chair. Measure this distance with the ruler and mark it around the entire chair with pins or chalk.

Planning Seam Lines

If the chair has squared-off back and arms, there must be a top back panel and top arm panels. For rounded back and arms, these are a matter of preference. If you decide to use them, consider how wide they should be and mark the outlines with pins, following the shape of the chair, or keeping lines straight with the help of the yardstick.

The side back panels may end at the top of the arms, at the top of the platform, or continue down to the top of the skirt. This will depend on the shape of the chair or may be a matter of individual taste. It is best to carry any side panels down as far as they will go, to avoid unnecessary seams; otherwise, mark the lines where they will end, measuring from the floor and keeping them straight.

The front arm panels may follow the lines of the upholstery or be planned for a simpler shape. Mark the outlines on the chair, making sure that the outlines of both front panels match; if necessary, make a paper

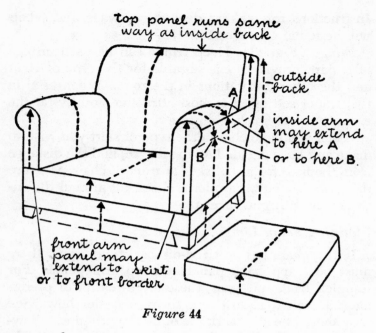

Figure **44**

pattern for one arm and reverse it for the other arm before marking them on chair.

If there is no top arm panel, there *must* be a seam between the inside and outside arm. This may be at A or at B on Fig. 44. For any fabric with an up and down design, it should be at A. To find this line, stand the yardstick upright against the arm and mark the point where it touches. Mark this point at front and back of arm, then use the yardstick to mark a straight line between these two points.

Straight of Goods

On all vertical parts of the chair, the lengthwise threads of the fabric should run *straight up and down from the floor*. Fig. 44 shows arrows to indicate the lengthwise grain. On the platform, cushion and on the top back panel, this lengthwise grain must run from front to back. On the top arm panels, the fabric will determine which way the pattern lies; any striped pattern must be matched to form a continuous stripe across each arm from the seat to the floor (Fig. 45). Stripes must also match from the top of the back to the seat, across the seat or cushion, and down the front to the floor. Stripes must also match at top of back, down the outside back to the floor. With a picture type of design, all the figures must be right side up on every section. Hold the fabric with the right side to you when placing it against the chair. In this way, you can see the pattern and decide how it will look best; it will also be easier to match stripes, plaids or other patterns. If you are using a solid color or a small all-over pattern, there will be no problem in placing the fabric except

Figure 45

Figure 46

to watch the grain carefully; but if there is a definite design, this must be centered on the major portions of the chair which must match one another when you are facing the chair.

Pinning and Cutting

If the fabric is folded, open it up and hold it with the right side to you and the wrong side against the chair (Fig. 46). *Before any cutting is done,* the fabric must be pinned each time to the section of the chair it is to cover. Don't let the extra yardage worry you—it can be pushed under the chair or to one side. By pinning and fitting before any cutting is done, there is less chance of error or of wasting material. Allow 2 inches for seams; this gives enough leeway for any adjustments when seams are pin-fitted. The tuck-in edges occur at the sides and back of the platform and may extend between the back and the inside arms. On special types of chairs there may be other tuck-in sections, so check carefully for these. It is possible to measure the depth of the tuck-in at any point by inserting a ruler into the channel (Fig. 47). In most cases, a 3-inch seam allowance at tuck-in joinings is ample for each section. When cutting, be sure to allow enough for these tuck-in edges.

Start by placing the fabric against the inside back. Center any design carefully and make certain the lengthwise grain runs up and down. Pin center of fabric to exact center line of back from top edge to platform; do not forget to leave the 2-inch margin around the top part and the 3-inch margin around all the portion that will be tucked in.

If you have one of the following chairs, check the special instructions given for these: *barrel-back chair,* or any chair with a curve around the back of the seat, on page 67; *channel-back chair* on page 67; *wing chair* on page 67.

Using plenty of pins, smooth the fabric toward the

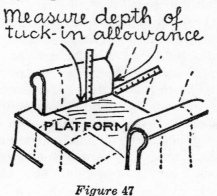

Figure 47

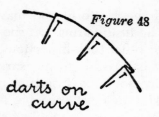

Figure 48

darts on curve

sides and corners. Pin from center to edges, placing pins close together around the edges.

If there is any fullness at edges or corners, pin tiny darts or make mitered corners (Fig. 48). If there is only slight fullness, this may be eased into the seam. Darts should match exactly on both sides. Fullness may also be gathered around a scroll-type curve (Fig. 49).

When the inside back has been firmly pinned and fitted, cut this piece off from the length of fabric, allowing for tuck-in and seam allowances. *Leave all pieces pinned to chair until every section has been cut and all seams pinned.* As soon as two adjoining pieces have been pinned to

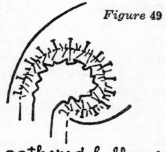

Figure 49

gathered fullness on scroll type curve

the chair and cut, pin the seams together as follows: Following the lines of the chair, bring the two edges together to form a clean seam line. You can feel the seam of the upholstery through the fabric. At corners and curves, where the outer edge of the seam allowance is too tight to follow the upholstery seam, it will be necessary to snip the edges—do not cut closer than ¼ inch of seam; it is better to make several small cuts than one long one (Fig. 50). Pins should be placed close together along the seam line and be firmly anchored so that they will not fall out. Keep straight

40

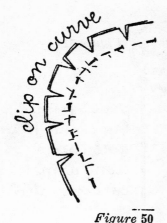

Figure 50

seams straight at all points, and curved seams smoothly curved. The 2-inch seam allowance will permit minor adjustments; take care that you do not pull any pieces out of line when pinning seams. It is better to have the cover slightly too large than the least bit too tight; even the finest fabric, or the welting, may shrink a fraction when it is first laundered or dry cleaned.

Now pin, cut and fit together the other sections of the back so that all pieces follow the lines of the chair. If there is an overhang on back or arms, fabric should fit under this curve and hug the upholstery at all points. Complete back, then the two arms. There is usually a slight variation in the two sides of a chair; since all upholstery is done by hand, and since the wear on any furniture is apt to be greater on one side than on the other, it is important to fit each side individually.

When joining inside arms to inside back, pin-fit the seam close to the seam of the chair until you reach the tuck-in. Wherever tuck-in edges join, flare the seam diagonally out to the corner, leaving only ½-inch seam allowance. When this portion of the tuck-in is pushed into the corner, it will have to spread out to lie flat. Unless it has sufficient width, it may ride up or rip. Next, pin platform and front border to other sections.

41

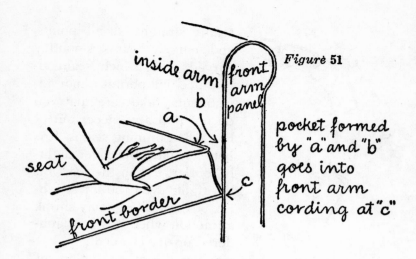

inside arm

b

a

front arm panel

Figure 51

seat

front border

c

pocket formed by "a" and "b" goes into front arm cording at "c"

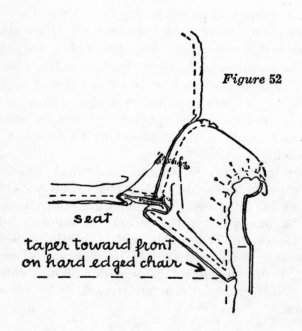

Figure 52

seat

taper toward front on hard edged chair →

On a spring-edge chair (Fig. 51), with a front edge that bends down when someone sits on it, there must be a "pocket" of tuck-in which will reach to the bottom of the space between the front border and the arm. One side of this pocket (a) is formed by joining the platform tuck-in allowance to the side of the front border; the other side of the pocket is formed by joining the tuck-in of the inside arm to the front arm panel (b). Below this pocket (c), the front border and front arm panel are joined together. The pocket allows enough play for the spring edge to be pushed down without tearing the slipcover away from the arm.

On a hard-edge chair (Fig. 52), there is no give to the front edge of the seat, which has only a padded, rigid frame. Here the tuck-in of platform is joined to the tuck-in of the inside arm, and it must be tapered off at the front so that it will fit into whatever space is provided by the padding. Too much excess fabric at this point will result in an ugly fold which cannot be hidden. If there is no tuck-in at all, sew welting around the back of the platform to make a finished seam.

Trimming and Notching the Seams

Check all the seams carefully to make certain that they fit smoothly. This is the time to make any adjustments by moving any pins that are out of line. Trim the 2-inch seam allowance to measure about ¾ inch (Fig. 53); the seam allowance should be exactly the same width on both thicknesses. Now spread open the seam allowance beyond the pins (Fig. 54) and mark both sides of the pinned seam with chalk or colored pencil *on the wrong side of fabric.* Do this on all seams.

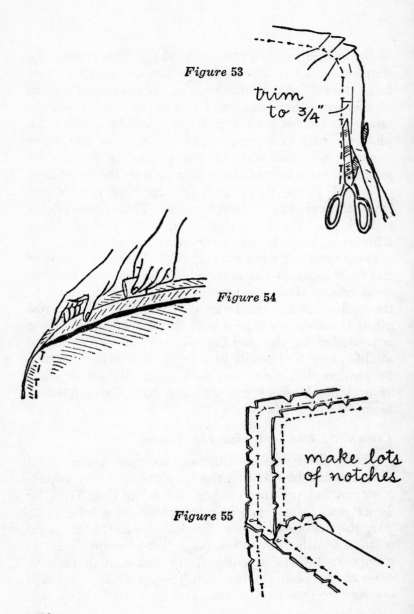

Figure 53

trim
to 3/4"

Figure 54

make lots
of notches

Figure 55

Next, make notches on all the seams, including the tuck-in edges. Fig. 55 shows how to make these notches; they should be about 3 or 4 inches apart on a long straight seam, closer together on a short or curved seam. Make different groupings of one, two or three notches for easy identification. By matching the notches, you will make sure that edges can be perfectly matched when sewing them together.

Cutting the Cushion

Place the fabric, right side up, on top of cushion. The lengthwise grain must run from front to back, and any pattern must be centered. Stripes should match those on the inside back and front border when the cushion is placed on chair. Pin fabric to cushion along the center line, then pin to side edges and corners at the seams of cushion. Leaving ½-inch seam allowance all around, cut away excess. Turn back seam allowance and mark the seam lines with chalk on the wrong side of fabric. Remove piece from cushion and mark the front edge on wrong side with "F." Cut another piece exactly the same size for reverse of cushion and mark seam lines and front edge to correspond.

If you have ever had a slipcover cut at home by a professional, you have probably seen the cutter leave with a large piece of uncut material neatly folded over one arm and have wondered whether he intended using your fabric to cover a chair of his own! If so, you have been accusing him unjustly—he has now completed all the work he can do at your house. When he returns to his shop, he will cut the other portions of the cushion cover and the slipcover skirt from

45

measurements. You, of course, will be able to do this at home.

Front Cushion Border: Measure the depth of the cushion at the front. Add 1 inch for seam allowance. Cut a piece to this measurement across the entire width of fabric. The front border will go across the front of the cushion and around both front corners as far as it will reach.

Back Borders: These may be cut on the length or width of the fabric. Cut two pieces the same width as front border and about 3 inches longer than zipper. Each piece will be folded in half, lengthwise, and the folds will meet at center of zipper. Remember you need the right length zipper for your particular cushion, as given on page 00.

Tail Strips: These will fill in the distance between the front and back borders and form a flap 3 inches deep over the zipper-pull. Cut two pieces same width as front border; one piece should be long enough to reach between front and back borders plus 1 inch for seams; the other piece should be 6 inches longer to allow for making the flap.

Cutting the Skirt

The various types of skirts are described on pages 31–35. The skirt must be cut so that the lengthwise grain of fabric runs up and down. Cut strips across the entire width of the material; each strip should be 3 inches deeper than the finished length of skirt to allow for seam and hem. When strips are seamed together, they will form a continuous strip for the skirt (except for simulated kick pleats).

Ruffled Skirts need from 2 to 3 times the circumference of the chair. Light-weight fabric needs more fullness than heavy fabric to avoid the appearance of being skimpy.

Box-Pleated or Knife-Pleated Skirts need 3 times the circumference of the chair.

Kick-Pleated Skirts need one width for each side of the chair; if fabric is narrow, you may require extra pieces inserted at each corner to make the kick pleats 3 or 4 inches deep; if the fabric is wide enough, each strip need only be as long as that side of the chair, plus 12 inches for making the pleats.

Simulated Kick Pleats require one width to fit each side, plus 1 inch for each side hem. They also need 3 flaps about 6 to 8 inches wide to go under the openings, and 2 flaps 4 inches wide for zipper opening edges.

The Skirt Lining sections are then cut to correspond, but each piece will be 3 inches shorter at lower edge. It can be cut on the width or the length of the goods.

To Cut and Make Self-Welting

Now that all the sections of the slipcover have been cut, any remnants can be used for self-welting. If there is 1 yard available, it will cover enough welting for the average chair. Smaller pieces can be pieced together; trim the edges evenly on the lengthwise grain, then sew these edges together on the wrong side and press the seams open. Fold one corner of the fabric with the crosswise grain meeting the lengthwise grain (Fig. 56), to get a true bias. Mark this fold with a pencil line. Open up the fabric with pencil line on top

47

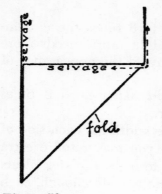

Figure 56

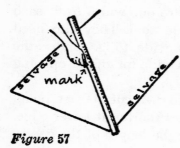

Figure 57

Figure 58

and lay the yardstick with one edge along this line (Fig. 57). Using the pencil, draw another line on the other side of the yardstick. Move the yardstick beyond the new line and draw another line on the other side. Continue to mark off diagonal lines about 1¼ inches apart, then cut along these lines to form bias strips (Fig. 58).

Sew bias strips together to form a continuous strip as follows: Place the diagonal end of one strip on the sewing machine, right side up. Place the end of the next strip, wrong side up, on top of it. Diagonal ends must meet so that strips will be at right angles to one another (Fig. 59). Sew these two ends together, but do not break off thread. Flip over the end of the second strip so that right side is uppermost and the free end is in position for sewing. Lay the next strip on top, wrong side up, and sew next seam. Continue in

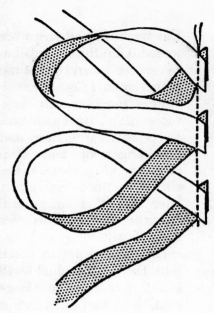

Place bias strips with right sides together join strips with one line of stitching, cut apart later

Figure 59

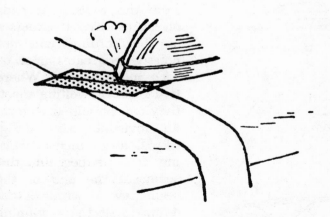

Figure 60

Figure 61

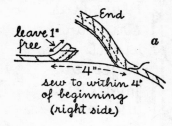

leave 1"
free

End

a

←- - -4"- - -→
*sew to within 4"
of beginning
(right side)*

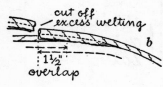

cut off
excess welting

b

1½"
overlap

rip stitching
on longer
end

c

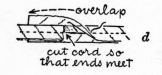

←- - - - -overlap

d

cut cord so
that ends meet

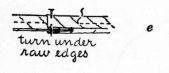

turn under
raw edges

e

welting

f

this way until all strips are joined. Clip the threads between seams and press the seams open (Fig. 60).

Fold the bias strip over the cording, right side out. Keep cord at center and raw edges of bias strip meeting. Stitch near the cord, but not too close; later the other seams will be stitched between this line of stitching and the cord. Be sure not to stitch into the cord, which will have to remain loose enough to be pulled out at the end of each seam. By removing 1 inch of cord from the welting at ends of seams, two thicknesses of the cording will not cross where seams meet.

To Splice Welting: Where two ends of welting meet, they can be joined to form an invisible seam (Fig. 61). Leave 1 inch of welting free at beginning of seam; at the end of the seam, sew to within about 4 inches of the beginning (a). Overlap the two ends by about 1½ inches and cut off excess welting (b). Rip the stitching that holds bias over the longer end and peel back the bias strip (c). Overlap ends and cut cord so that the two ends of cord will just meet (d). Turning under the raw edge, wrap the free end of bias around the short end (e). Check the welting now, to see that it is exactly the right length to finish seam (f). Stitch in place on right side. This splicing must be done on cushion cover.

To Finish Off End of Welting. Cut welting 1 inch beyond end of seam. Peel back the bias strip from this end for about 2 inches and cut off 1 inch of cord. Fold under raw edge of bias to correct length and finish seam.

Sewing the Slipcover

The zipper opening will be on one side of the outside back and will extend from about 2 inches below top of chair to lower edge of skirt. Select the side that will be the least conspicuous, depending on the position of the chair in the room, and mark this side for opening.

Mark each section of slipcover, with a small piece of paper pinned securely with a safety pin, for identification: left outside arm, right outside arm, etc. Remove the pins that hold the fabric to the upholstery, but leave seams pinned together and the cover on chair. Remove only one piece at a time, and when you do, mark the reverse side with chalk, "F" for front or "T" for top. These precautions will be of help should you forget which edges go together, especially if there is no right or wrong side to the fabric. As

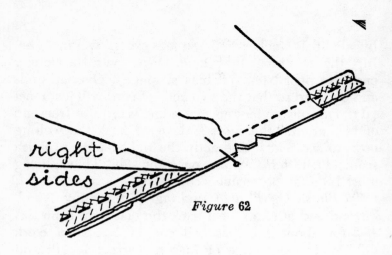

right
sides

Figure 62

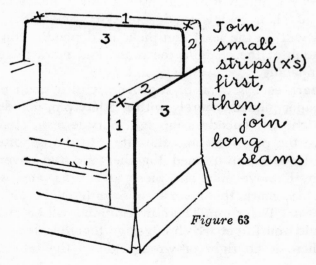

Join
small
strips(x's)
first,
then
join
long
seams

Figure 63

pieces are removed, sew any darts or make any gathers before removing the next piece.

Unpin the outside back first. Sew welting around top and side edges as follows: Allow enough free welting on zipper opening side to reach to the floor, plus a couple of inches for finishing. Leave the welting on this side free; later, it must be joined to the opposite edge of zipper opening, where it will conceal the zipper from the side view of the chair.

Place welting in sewing position on the machine, with the cording at left and raw edges at right. Now place the edge of the outside back on top of cording, wrong side up. Raw edge of back will be over raw edges of welting. The chalk-marked seam line will be in plain view and you can feel the cording, which should be kept close to the seam (Fig. 62). Sew welting around sides and top, *except along zipper opening*. Cut off excess welting and remove 1 inch of cord from the end.

When joining the next piece, you must decide which side of the seam will have the welting sewn to it and which seams will be welted first. *Never try to sew a seam and put in the welting at the same time;* the welting is always sewn to one edge first. Figs. 63 and 64 show two different types of chairs. The welting is sewn first to the shorter seams, which join sections 1 and 2, *so that longer welted seam can be made last* with the welting in one continuous piece on the edge of section 3.

To join the next piece to the welted edge, pin both sections with right sides together and the welting between them, matching all notches exactly. Place them on the machine with the new piece underneath and the

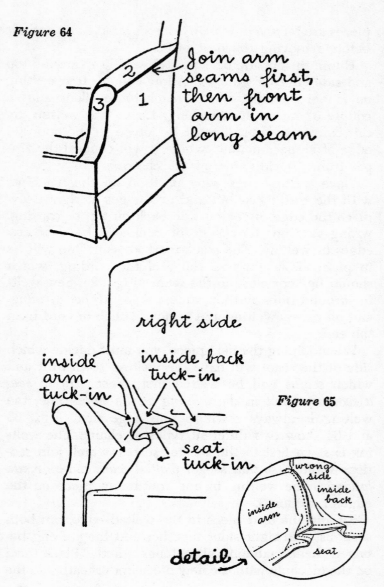

Figure 64

Join arm seams first, then front arm in long seam

2

3   1

right side

inside arm tuck-in

inside back tuck-in

Figure 65

seat tuck-in

detail ➤

wrong side

inside back

inside arm

seat

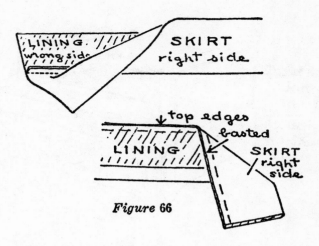

Figure 66

previous stitching line on top. Stitch *just inside* the previous stitching line.

Join all sections of the back first, then the sections of one arm at a time. Replace these pieces on the chair and pin them together where they meet, being sure to *flare* the corners of the tuck-in (Fig. 65). Next, sew the platform and front border in place, remembering that these are joined differently for a hard-edge chair and a spring-edge chair (see page 42).

When all sections have been joined, place the slip-cover on the chair. Pin the zipper opening together; zipper cannot be inserted until the skirt has been completed. Measure the line for top of skirt from the floor and mark this line with chalk around the entire cover. On a chair with a rounded front, mark the position of front legs as a guide in making kick-pleats. Sew welting around marked line, making sure that it will meet at edges of zipper opening.

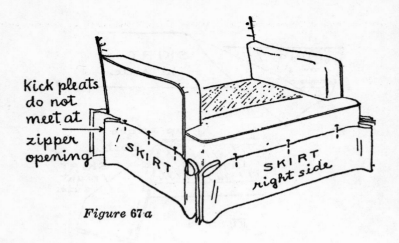

Kick pleats
do not
meet at
zipper
opening

SKIRT

SKIRT
right side

Figure 67a

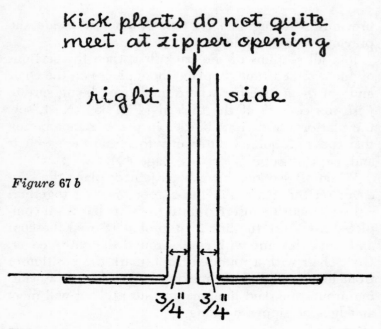

Kick pleats do not quite
meet at zipper opening

right   side

Figure 67 b

3/4" 3/4"

Sewing the Skirt

Except for simulated kick pleats, which are described later, sew skirt sections together. Press seams open. Place lining and skirt with right sides together and sew bottom seam ½ inch from edge (Fig. 66). Turn piece right side out and bring other long edges together; since lining is shorter, this will form the hem. Press hem. Now pin the skirt to cover, starting at edge of zipper opening; leave ¾ inch perfectly flat—without pleats or gathers—on each side of opening for sewing in zipper.

Ruffled Skirt: Run at least 4 rows of stitching around top to hold cording. Draw up cording, gathering fullness evenly on each side and hiding the seams in the ruffles. Instructions for attaching skirt are given later.

Kick-Pleated Skirt: Pin the center of each width to center of back, front or side, then carry the fullness to the corners to form pleats, keeping pleats ¾ inch from zipper edges (Fig. 67 a and b). In this way, seams will fall under pleats.

Other Pleated One-Piece Skirts: Distribute pleats evenly on each side of chair, hiding seams under pleats. Pin any pleats at top and bottom and mark position of pleats on cover with notches. Remove skirt, then remove cover from chair. Place skirt on a flat surface and check any pleats so that they lie straight with grain of fabric and edges are even at top and bottom. Baste.

Attaching Skirt: Pin skirt to slipcover, right sides together, either with ruffles evenly distributed or with pleats at notches. Remember to leave ¾ inch flat on each side of zipper opening, having hemlines meeting

Figure 68

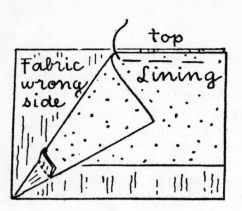

top

Fabric wrong side

Lining

a

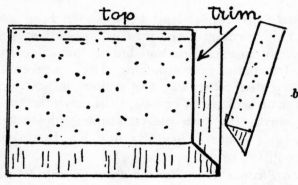

top

trim

b

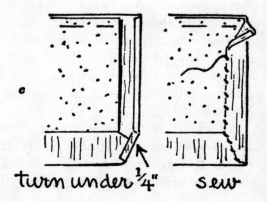

c

turn under ¼"

sew

58

at base of opening. Baste skirt to cover, try it on chair to see how it hangs, then stitch skirt in place.

Simulated Kick Pleats: Line each section of skirt separately by placing lining and fabric with right sides together and sewing bottom seam ½ inch from edge. Turn piece right side out and baste top edges together, forming hem (Fig. 68a). Press. Mark side edges so that each section will fit the side of chair for which it is intended, having about 1 inch on each side for hems; at each side of zipper opening, skirt should reach to within ¼ inch of seamline. Cut off side seam allowance on lining (Fig. 68b) from top edge to top of hem, then cut diagonally to corner of hem. Turn under ¼ inch of hem allowance and baste. Baste corner diagonally. Cut off excess at corner (c), then turn hem allowance over lining and sew in place by hand (d).

Pin skirt sections to slipcover, making sure that hems meet exactly at corners and are even at zipper opening. Stitch in place. Line flaps in the same way. Pin the 4-inch flaps under skirt at edges of zipper opening, filling in the ¼ inch that was left free (Fig. 69). Pin

Figure 69

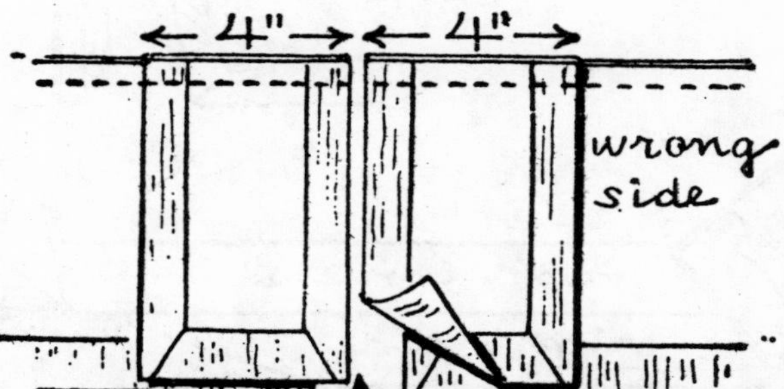

zipper opening

59

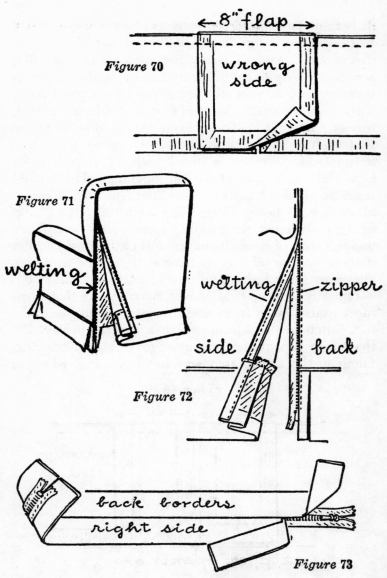

← 8" flap →

Figure 70

wrong side

Figure 71

welting

welting

zipper

side

back

Figure 72

back borders

right side

Figure 73

the other flaps under corners, centering them under each opening (Fig. 70). All flaps should be ½ inch shorter than skirt, so that the corners will not show. Sew flaps to cover.

Insert Zipper: Sew the free end of welting to the *side* edge of cover, making sure it does not pucker where it crosses over from the back edge, and finishing off the end neatly at skirt hem (Fig. 71). Pin the closed zipper, right side up, under welted edge with pull-tab at bottom of opening. Welting should cover one half of zipper teeth. Turn under seam allowance on other edge and pin to other side of zipper with fold meeting welting at center of zipper. Check again to make certain that ends of welting will meet at top of skirt and that hem edges are even (Fig. 72). Stitch zipper in place from right side, stitching just inside welting on the one edge and ¼ inch from fold on other edge. Stitch firmly across top. Press slipcover.

Finish Raw Edges: This is optional. Edges can be lock-stitched, overcast by hand or bound with tape.

Sewing Cushion Cover

Sew welting around edge of top section, splicing the ends neatly at center back (see page 50). Fold the two back border sections in half lengthwise, right side out. Place the two folded edges over closed zipper so that folds meet at center; zipper must be right side out (Fig. 73). Pin, then stitch ¼ inch from center of zipper and across both ends.

With right sides together, pin tail-strips to ends of zipper piece with longer tail-strip at end with pull-tab. Keeping seams straight across grain on each section, stitch twice across about 1 inch beyond ends of zipper

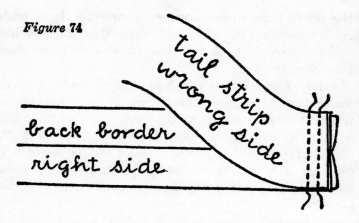

Figure 74

tail strip
wrong side

back border
right side

(Fig. 74). The two rows of stitching will hold these two seams securely. Fold the longer tail-strip to form a 3-inch flap over zipper-pull, then stitch edges of flap to hold them in place (Fig. 75). This fold will cover the tab and eliminate any possible friction against back of chair.

Find center front of cushion top and center of front border. Remember that front border must *never* have seams. Pin these with right sides together, then pin front border across front and around front corners as far as it will go, leaving ½ inch free for seams. Pin back border and tail-strips across back of cushion top and around sides to meet front border. Allowing for seams, cut off excess. Sew ends of border sections together, making sure that seams are on straight of goods, otherwise borders will slant. Sew borders to cushion top. *Open zipper,* so that when other side is sewn in place, it will be possible to turn cover right side out.

Make a notch at each corner of border where it meets top. Fold border across straight of goods at each notch and notch other edge (see Fig. 75). These notches must be directly opposite one another.

Sew welting around reverse of cushion, splicing it at center back. Starting at left front corner, pin other edge of borders to this piece, making sure that notches are at corners so that border will lie straight between the two pieces. Sew in place. Turn cover right side out and insert cushion.

Barrel-Back Chairs (see Figs. 7 and 10 on page 16).

Pinning Inside Back: When pinning fabric to the inside curve of back, do not stretch it across; leave it loose enough so that it will hug the entire surface from side to side when stitched to the adjoining pieces at top and bottom. If it is too tight, the sides will be pulled forward and out of line, and the seams are apt to rip if someone leans back against it. Use extra pins to hold it against the upholstery.

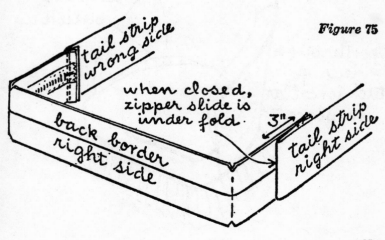

Figure 75

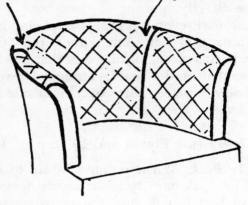

Back sections joined first

Figure 76

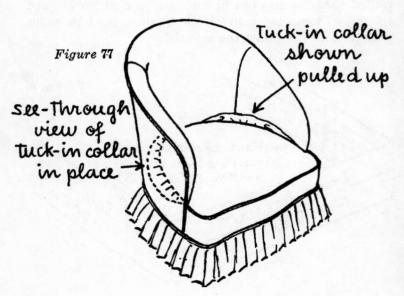

Figure 77

Tuck-in collar
shown
pulled up

see-Through
view of
tuck-in collar
in place

If the chair is a *wide barrel-back* (Fig. 76), the width of the curve may require more than one width of fabric. There should *never* be a center seam; always center the fabric on both the inside and outside back, then join two pieces to this center section, matching any pattern. Pin the center section first, then decide how wide this should be so that the seams will fall in the most suitable place. Unless the pattern determines the position of these seams, it is best to space them so that they will not be too close to the sides. The seams on the outside back should match those on inside back.

Top Border: If there is a top back border, it must be curved to correspond with the top of the chair. Never try to fit a straight piece around the top; lay the fabric flat across the entire curve and pin it at both edges to follow the lines of the chair.

Collar for Tuck-In: A separate flange must be made for barrel-back chairs, or any chairs that have a curve around the back of the seat, so that the tuck-in will be wide enough to spread into the curved space. The extra length, allowed on straight-backed chairs, would not flare enough to fit. There are two types of collars:

Pleated Collar (Fig. 77): Measure the distance around the inside edge of seat where tuck-in occurs. Cut a strip of fabric about 4 inches wide and twice the length of this measurement. Pin ½-inch tucks, 1 inch apart, along both edges, with the tucks facing in the same direction on each edge. Stitch tucks in place at each edge (Fig. 78a). If the tuck-in tapers off to nothing at the front edge of the chair, taper the stitching to meet at both ends of collar (b). Find center of collar. Pin

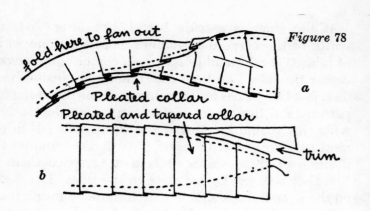

fold here to fan out

Pleated collar

Pleated and tapered collar

trim

Figure 78

a

b

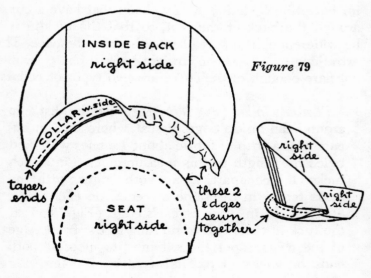

INSIDE BACK
right side

Figure 79

COLLAR w.side

taper
ends

SEAT
right side

these 2
edges
sewn
together

right
side

right
side

center of one tucked edge to center of inside back, then pin remainder of same edge along inside back. Pin other edge to platform. The center of collar will spread out like a fan and reach into the tuck-in space. Stitch in place; if tuck-in tapers at front, cut off excess at edges.

Fitted Collar (Fig. 79): Make a paper pattern of the curve around back and sides of seat. This curve will be the inside curve (short curve) of collar. Collar should be about 4 inches wide. Cut collar from pattern and sew short curve to inside back. If tuck-in tapers to nothing at front edge, taper ends of collar to correspond. A regular 3-inch allowance for tuck-in is made when cutting the platform, then this edge is sewed to long edge of collar. Again, this seam allowance may have to be tapered to fit at front edge.

Channel-Back Chairs (See Fig. 9 on page 16.)

Pinning Inside Back: Pin lengthwise grain of fabric straight up and down at center. Tuck fabric into each groove, keeping it smooth and pinning it in place from top to bottom between grooves. At lower edge, slash fabric along center of each groove for about 3 inches; the excess fullness is then taken in by a dart that tapers to nothing above the slash. Make darts at upper edge to correspond. Baste all darts and try cover on chair before stitching. Pin in place on chair before cutting other sections.

Wing Chairs (See Fig. 6 on page 15.)

The inside wings must match one another. Since various views of a wing chair will show an inside and

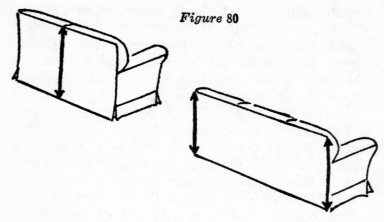

Figure 80

outside arm or wing at the same time, it is best if they all match one another. Follow the outlines of the chair carefully. There is usually a tuck-in where the wings join the inside back; if so, measure the depth of this space and allow this measurement plus ½ inch for seams. Taper this tuck-in allowance as necessary for proper fit.

Overstuffed Sofas and Love Seats

The method for making slipcovers for sofas is simi-ᴌar to that for overstuffed chairs. The major difference is the greater width on seat and back, each of which requires more than one width of fabric. A two-seat sofa will need two widths of material with a seam at the center; a three-seat sofa will need three widths and two seams. Check the types of sofas on pages 19–21 and select the one that most closely resembles yours. This picture will show the seams where sections meet. See yardage chart on page 245.

In most cases the two-seat sofa will need only one

zipper. The zipper opening can be made at center seam on outside back where the two widths meet, or it can be at one back corner if the sofa has straight sides. The three-seat sofa needs two zippers, one at each back corner (Fig. 80). There must also be one zipper for each cushion (see page 27 for information about zippers and other materials needed). The seams on any top back border and front border must be lined up with the seams on inside back, and each section of these should have any pattern centered. If there are no cushions, the pattern must be centered on each seat section, and the seams must meet those on inside back. All of these seams, except on the seat, should be welted.

For a kick-pleated skirt, there should be a kick pleat at each seam (Fig. 81).

Most sofas have seam lines on the upholstery, but if the fabric on the back is in one continuous piece, then

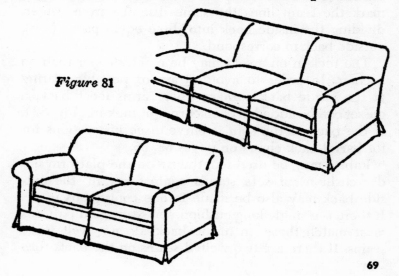

Figure 81

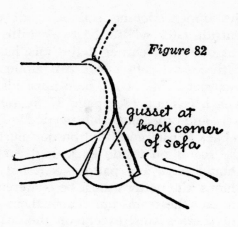

Figure 82

gusset at
back corner
of sofa

find the exact center of back. Fasten a string to the
top at this point, carry it down to platform, across
platform and straight down to lower edge of front.
Fasten securely at exact center. If there is only one
seam, this will mark its position; if there are two seams,
mark the seam lines the same distance from center,
dividing the inside back into three equal parts. Mark
outside back to correspond.

The tuck-in on a sofa may be much deeper than on
a chair. In order to avoid strain or possible tearing
at the inside back corners where arms meet back, a
gusset can be added at each corner of tuck-in (Fig. 82).
If the back of the sofa is curved, see instructions for
for barrel-back chairs on pages 63, 65.

Fabric may be used lengthwise on the platform under cushions; if sofa stands against a wall, the outside back may also be made in one continuous piece.
If there is a single long cushion, the seams and patterns
must match those on inside back; do not welt these
seams. If there are two welted seams on the back, turn

the welting toward the sides when sewing back to adjoining sections.

Proceed as for overstuffed chairs; when cutting cushion covers fit each one separately: cut the top, then cut the reverse to match and pin them to the cushion for which they are intended. No two cushions are exactly the same. When each cushion cover is completed, put it on the cushion for which it was made. When removing these covers for cleaning, mark each cushion and each cover, so that they will be replaced correctly.

FURNITURE WITH WOODEN FRAMES

There are several types for which you may wish to make slipcovers:

1. Straight chair with open back (Fig. 83)
2. Occasional chair with open back and arms (Fig. 84)
3. Side chair with closed back (Fig. 85)
4. Armchair with closed back and open arms (Fig. 86)
5. Armchair with closed back and arms (Fig. 87)

Any of these types may be fitted with one-piece slipcovers similar to those for overstuffed furniture (Fig. 88). When back or arms are open, each section may have a separate cover (Fig. 89).

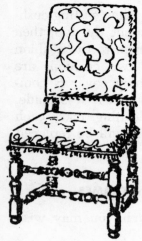

Figure 83

Figure 84

Figure 85

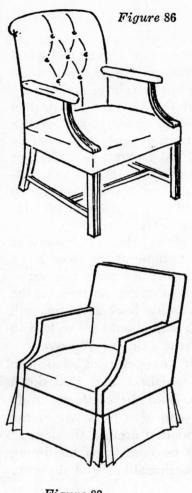

Figure 86

Figure 87

Figure 88

Figure 89

One-Piece Slipcovers

Pad the top of the back frame with a strip of flannel, cotton batting or foam rubber taped over the wood (Fig. 90). This will serve two purposes: it will form a base to which you can pin the fabric, and it may be left on the frame, under the slipcover, to protect the fabric from sharp edges or carvings and give a smoother line. Protruding knobs or posts can either be padded and covered with fitted sections (Fig. 91), or left bare by making openings (Fig. 92). When padding has been taped in place, cut a 3-inch or 4-inch strip of fabric across the width of goods and pin this along the padded edge (Fig. 93).

When back and arms are closed, the tuck-in may be rather shallow and taper to nothing at the front edge. For a shallow tuck-in, 2½ inches for seam allowance will usually be ample. Where there is no tuck-in, the seam where platform meets inside back and arms will follow the lines of the chair and should be welted to correspond with the other seams on the slipcover.

A one-piece slipcover for an open-back chair can have a tuck-in allowance, which is later tied down with tape under the seat to hold the platform firmly in place (Fig. 94). Tapes can also be sewn to the inside corners of border and tied around the legs of the chair. This is especially recommended for dining room chairs, which are uncomfortable if the slipcover shifts.

One-piece slipcovers for straight chairs need no opening. However, if the back or arms flare beyond the seat (Fig. 95), make a zipper opening at one back corner.

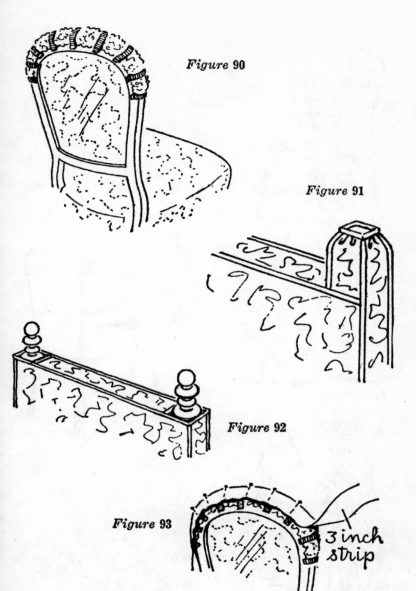

Figure 90

Figure 91

Figure 92

Figure 93

3 inch
strip

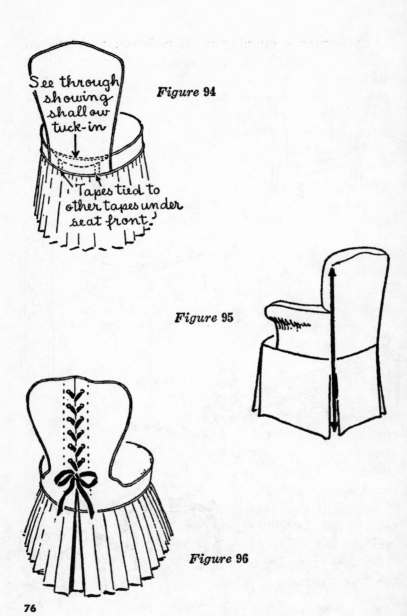

See through
showing
shallow
tuck-in

Figure 94

Tapes tied to
other tapes under
seat front

Figure 95

Figure 96

An attractive opening for a bedroom or Victorian chair, especially one that is used in front of a dressing table or desk, can be made as in Fig. 96. Make two separate sections for the outside back, allowing 2 inches for center hem on each side. Sew these sections together for about 2 inches from top, hem remainder of center edges. Pierce these hems from top seam to "waistline" of chair, making eyelets about 2 inches apart and directly opposite one another. Back sections are then laced together with tape, ribbon or narrow bands of self-fabric which are tied in a bow at "waistline." For underlap, cut a strip of fabric about 3 inches wide and long enough to fit under entire back opening. Hem the edges, then sew one edge in place under hem and fasten the other edge under the opposite hem with snap tape.

Instead of making two sections, it is also possible to make a deep inverted pleat down the back; make eyelets in the folds of the pleat and lace the folds together. The pleat must be wide enough to provide room for removing the slipcover.

In order to fit snugly, a one-piece slipcover should have a border around the lower edge of the seat. This can be a separate piece, or the skirt can be held tight to simulate a border by shirring a ruffled skirt with 4-cord shirring tape, or by stitching any pleats firmly in place for about 4 inches. Tapes to hold the seat of the cover in place can be attached on the wrong side at the base of this border, or simulated border, and tied around the chair legs. Proceed as for overstuffed chairs.

Sew welting around
inside + outside back

Figure 97

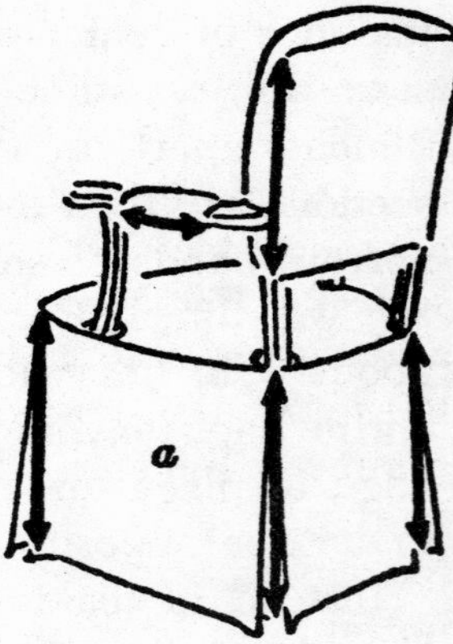

Figure 98

b

a

Back
skirt

Side skirt

Side skirt

Seat

Border

Front skirt

78

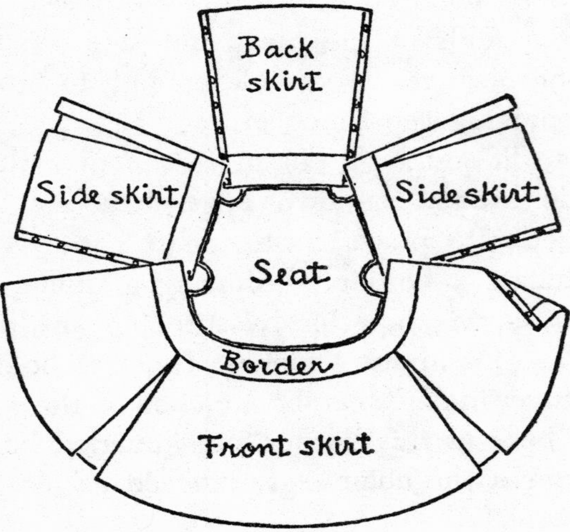

Separate Sections for Back, Seat and Arms

Since these fit more closely than one-piece slip-covers, they are especially recommended for formal rooms. Cover the top edge of back frame with a strip of flannel, cotton batting or foam rubber taped in place (see Fig. 93 on page 75). Cut a 3-inch or 4-inch strip of fabric across width of goods and pin this piece along top of padding for top border. The border will extend down the sides to the base of the back (Fig. 97), or to the arms. For a chair with open arms, another piece will make the border below arms to seat. Pin, cut and pin-fit the inside and outside back as for overstuffed furniture. Back sections will extend to the open edge at base of back and should be welted around all edges. If an opening is needed for the back, use either a zipper or snap tape. The skirt of the slipcover must have openings at each post (wooden upright) of back and arms (Fig. 98 a and b), with all the openings overlapping from front to back. Since all of these openings must open all the way, the only zippers that can be used are jacket-type zippers. These must be the exact length of the skirt, or slightly shorter, and the zipper-pull should be at the lower edge where it will be least noticeable. Turn the zipper tape underneath at top and also at lower edge if it will show. Snap tape can be used on these openings.

Sewing On Snap Tape: Sew tape underneath front edge for overlap. Both sides of tape must be sewed down so the tape will not pull away from opening. On the overlap, stitch outer edge; sew inner edge by hand so it will not show. The tape on underlap is stitched on right side at both the edges. Check to be certain

79

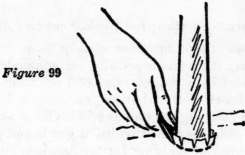

Figure 99

Figure 100

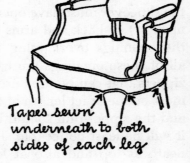

Figure 101

Tapes sewn underneath to both sides of each leg

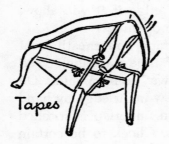

Tapes

Figure 102

that snaps will meet, and tuck the raw ends underneath. Tape should be close to the edge to avoid any gaping of seams.

The seat must be fitted around the posts; clip seam allowance as necesary to bring fabric tight against the wood and mark seam line with chalk (Fig. 99). Sew welting around the seam lines on each of these openings. Raw edges of welting and fabric are then turned to wrong side and covered with a bias strip, sewed in place by hand. Proceed with seat, border and skirt as for overstuffed chairs. Small separate covers are made for the upholstered sections on arms (Fig. 100). Make a section for top, then welt both side edges. The ends may need darts to follow the contour of padding. Add two sections to reach under the arm and overlap. Hem bottom edges, sew welting across both ends. Fasten with snap tape.

Ending Off Slipcovers Under Seat of Chair

Some slipcovers are made to end under the bottom rails of the chair, omitting any skirt or flounce. The lower edge of the border should follow the line of the chair if this is shaped (Fig. 101). Finish the lower edge with welting, which should be even with edge of lower rail. This edge can now be held in place as follows:

1. Sew a tape to edge of slipcover on each side of the legs. Stretch the tapes diagonally across bottom of chair (Fig. 102) and tie at center.
2. Try cover on chair and mark each edge where it meets the legs on each side. Sew a 4-inch strip

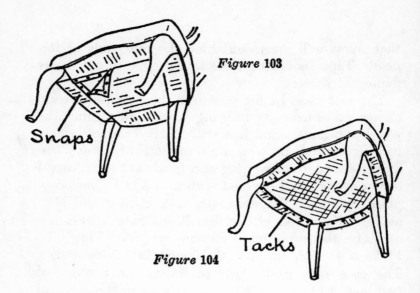

Figure 103

Snaps

Tacks

Figure 104

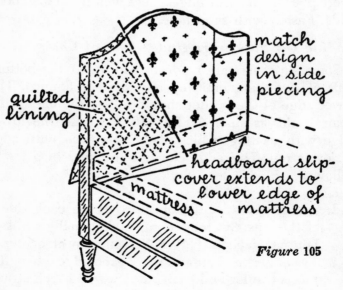

quilted
lining

match
design
in side
piecing

headboard slip-
cover extends to
lower edge of
mattress

mattress

Figure 105

of fabric between markers, hemming the ends of each strip. Hem free long edges. These free edges can now be fastened together with diagonal tapes, or they can be snap-taped to a piece of muslin that will fit under the bottom of the chair (Fig. 103). They can also be tacked to bottom rails (Fig. 104). Keep them drawn snugly so that they will not show.

SLIPCOVERS FOR HEADBOARDS

A slipcover for a headboard to match the curtains or bedspread will transform a bedroom completely. The one-piece slipcover is the easiest to make and will fit any kind of headboard. Metal headboards should have a covering of flannel or quilting made to fit under the slipcover. Use quilted lining material or a discarded quilt or blanket to make this (Fig. 105). First, tape a strip of cotton batting, flannel or thin foam rubber along the edge of the frame (see Fig. 93 on page 75), to which the fabric can be pinned. Cut a strip of fabric about 4 or 5 inches wide and pin it across the top of the headboard over the taped padding. Pin-fit and cut the pieces carefully, as for overstuffed furniture. The headboard cover should extend far enough so that the lower edge will be hidden by the mattress. Cut a length of fabric for the center, then add strips on each side, matching any pattern, to make headboard cover desired width. Sew welting around this piece. Back section will not show, so it can be made of muslin. Sew border to front, then sew welting around opposite side of border. If the headboard flares, the cover may need a zipper opening at

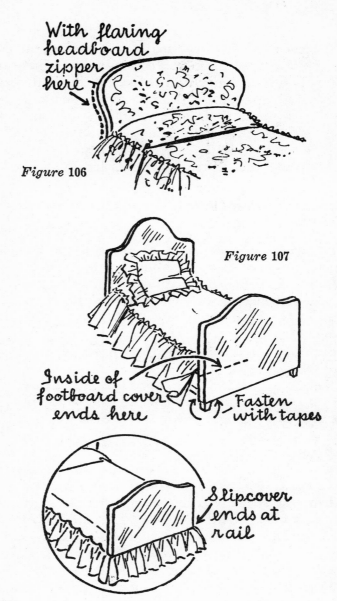

With flaring headboard zipper here →

Figure 106

Figure 107

Inside of footboard cover ends here

Fasten with tapes

Slipcover ends at rail

Figure 108

one back corner (Fig. 106). Sew back section in place and hem lower edge.

A footboard can be covered to correspond. When the footboard extends below the box spring, the outside of the cover will be longer than the inner section. Both sides of the footboard must be seamed with patterns matching and have welting around the tops and sides. Make the border long enough to reach to bottom of outside section and sew the pieces together. Hem lower edges. Fasten the ends of the border around the legs of the bed with tape (Fig. 107).

Short posts can also be covered to match the headboard. Make these in sections (Fig. 108) with welting between the sections. The top can be square or round to fit the post, or be omitted on a tapered post. Any opening is closed with snap tape.

$\mathscr{D}$raperies

Window treatments should always be planned with several purposes in mind:

Control of Light: Sunny windows and bedroom windows will need blinds, window shades, shutters or draw draperies to keep out excessive sunshine.

Privacy: Whereas a penthouse or a cabin in the woods may not require window shades, the average house or apartment is close enough to its neighbors so that windows need some sort of curtaining to insure privacy, especially after dark when the rooms are illuminated.

Decoration: Windows may be as simple or as formal as you wish; they can have straight-hanging draperies to match the wall or be dramatized with swags. The fabric can be calico or satin, the color neutral or brilliant. This depends on your personal preference and the suitability for the rest of your decor.

Proportion: Curtains can change the proportions of a room. They can make it look larger, wider, higher or smaller. They can cover a group of windows or a whole wall; they can mask architectural faults and problem windows or window groupings.

Dramatizing or Hiding the View: If a picture window looks out over a garden, hillside or lake, draw draperies can be placed so that none of the view is obscured. On the other hand, if the window opens into a courtyard or on your neighbor's garage or clothesline, sheer glass curtains will screen the view without shutting out the light.

Temperature Control: North windows or those exposed to the wind can be covered with lined draperies to keep out drafts and hold in the heat. Psychologically, full-length draperies will make a cold room appear warmer, whereas sheer curtains or bamboo blinds will give a feeling of coolness. A change of curtains for different seasons is an excellent practice and one you may decide to try. By making them yourself, you can probably have two sets for the price of one.

Appearance from the Outside: It has been said that the architect who builds a house should be allowed to plan the window treatments. In an apartment building where each tenant has different taste and furnishings, this may not be of prime importance; but in a one-family house, the total effect is spoiled if the curtains are out of keeping with the architectural style. Ruffled organdy is attractive for a Colonial cottage but unsuitable for an Italian villa; café curtains are appropriate for a modern house but look out of place against Victorian windows. Pink ruffled curtains at one window, flowered chintz at another and café curtains at a third may harmonize with a bedroom, living room and dinette, but from the street they will look disorganized and patchy. To maintain unity, all the windows on one floor should have blinds of the same color or draperies lined with a neutral tone to hide the

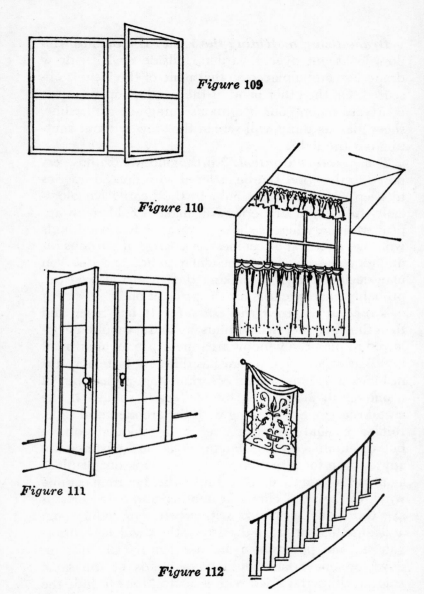

Figure 109

Figure 110

Figure 111

Figure 112

variations that can then be carried out in different rooms.

Look at the illustrations in this section and decide which of the various window treatments will go best with the type of windows and other decorations in your rooms. Remember that curtains should never be skimpy; if your budget is limited, it is better to buy a bolt of unbleached muslin than a few yards of hand-blocked linen; it is better to make café curtains with enough fullness to hang gracefully than to have narrow full-length draperies. Long curtains with insufficient fullness look stringy and cheapen the appearance of any room. Always plan from two to three times the width of the window area the curtains are to cover. The thinner the fabric, the more fullness is necessary.

There are several kinds of windows that will influence your choice:

Windows that open into the room (Fig. 109): The curtains must draw out of the way so that they will not interfere with the windows.

Dormer windows (Fig. 110): The curtains must fit within the dormer.

French doors (Fig. 111): The glass may be covered with sheer curtains stretched between top and bottom rods. If the doors open outward, add draw draperies that can be pulled aside when the doors are opened or will open with the doors. Front doors with glass panels and the narrow windows that frequently flank them can also be curtained in this way.

Stairway windows (Fig. 112): Except in the most formal houses, where draperies may sweep down to

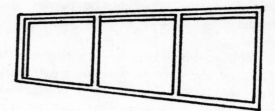

Figure 113

touch the steps, it is best to use shutters, a decorative window shade or curtains that hang within the window frame.

Windows set high in the wall (Fig. 113): If these are not needed for light, they can be painted to match the walls and look like recesses. Often they need no curtaining at all; glass shelves with potted plants or a collection of interesting bottles will turn them into decorative niches. In modern houses, café curtains, shutters or sill-length curtains are customarily used.

Windows close to a corner: If there is no room for draperies to match those at the other windows, a half-drapery can be used (Fig. 114), or rods that are butted together at the corner can carry part of the drapery along the other wall (Fig. 115).

Window seat alcoves or bay windows: Each window can be curtained separately (Fig. 116), or draperies can be hung on a ceiling track in front of the bay (Fig. 117) or on a custom-made curved track in front of the curtains.

Fig. 118 shows how horizontal lines will make a room look wider. The tops of the windows can be covered with a short valance or with a cornice painted to match the walls; café curtains across the entire width will emphasize the horizontal effect.

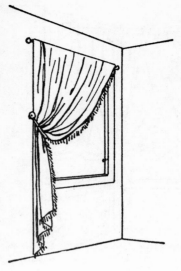

Figure 114

Figure 115

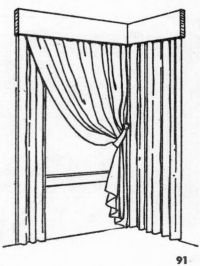

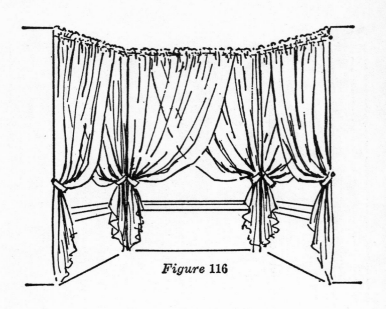

Figure 116

Figure 117

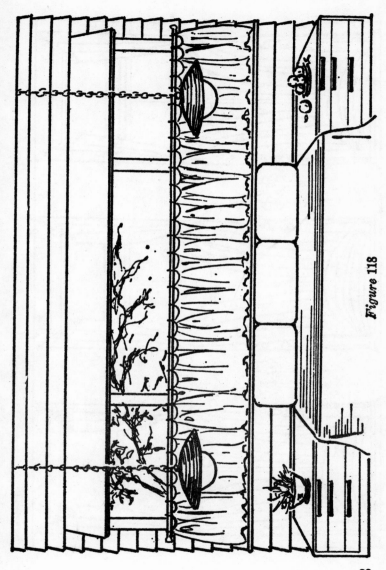

Figure 118

93

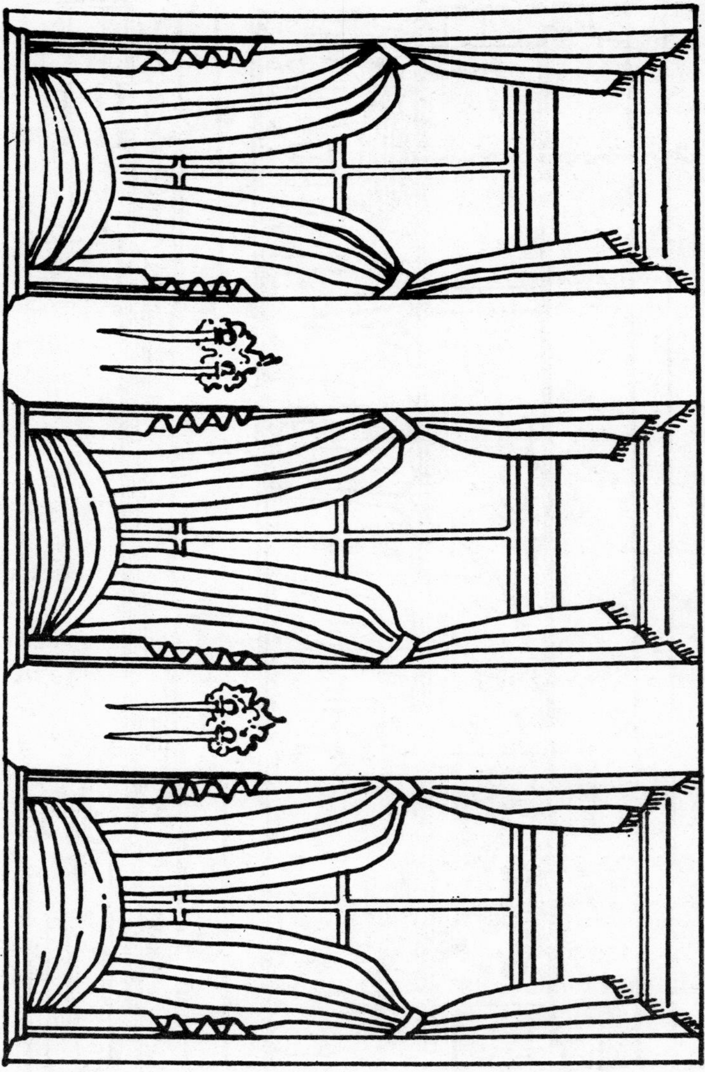

Figure 119

Fig. 119 illustrates how a ceiling can be made to look higher. Start the curtains at the ceiling and bring them all the way to the floor. Accentuate the vertical lines by curtaining each window separately. An interesting top treatment will also carry the eye toward the top of the windows and give a feeling of height.

Fig. 120 is an example of making a room appear larger by curtaining an entire wall from ceiling to floor and from side to side. The large expanse of curtains, when drawn across the windows, seems to enlarge the whole area. For a room with no windows, or very small windows, this type of curtaining will create the illusion of a picture window.

In Fig. 121, curtains are used to cover two windows of different sizes and to treat them as a single unit.

Always remember that vertical lines accentuate height, horizontal lines accentuate the width. The pattern of a fabric, especially stripes, can also be used to produce these effects.

We have tried to include all of the information you will need to duplicate any type of window treatment that can be executed by the home decorator with the possible assistance of her home handyman in attaching fixtures and valance boards.

HOW TO DETERMINE DRAPERY HARDWARE NEEDED

Study the sketches given here to determine which sort of hardware to choose. It is best to purchase and install your brackets, rods or traverse rods before you measure the lengths of material that are needed for your window curtains or draperies. This procedure makes your sewing easier as you then know exactly the

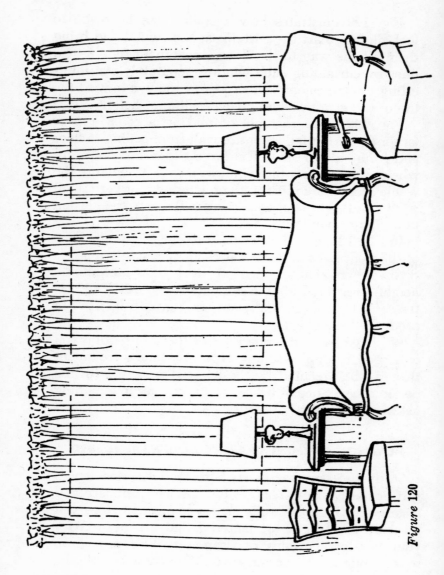

Figure 120

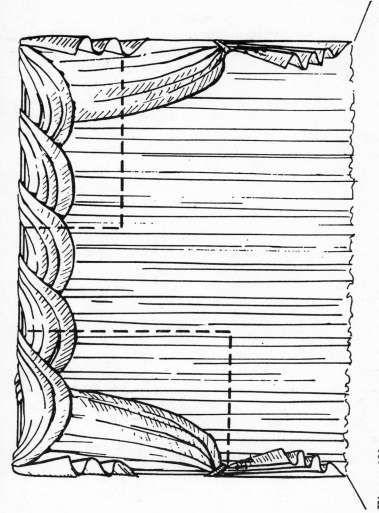

Figure 121

lengths to cut, what your hem allowances will be, the depth of headings or pleats that will look best and the clearance the draperies will need to draw across the rods when you wish to close them. These sketches will give you an indication of what is available when you go to your drapery, department store or fixture shop.

Adjustable Traverse Rod, Fig. 122: Has a center-close two-way draw. Length: This simplest of all traverse rods comes in 28 to 48 inches and in 48 to 86 inches. These dimensions are the minimum and maximum lengths to which the rod will extend.

Overlap, Fig. 123: When the traverse draperies are drawn together, one panel should overlap the other panel by about 3 inches to insure nighttime privacy or to close out excessive sunlight in those parts of the country where midday sunlight is too strong.

Projection, Fig. 124: This is the distance the rod projects from the wall into the room. Short projections are available for glass curtains, longer ones for draperies.

Return, Fig. 125: The distance from the front of the rod to the wall or window casing where the bracket is fastened. This "return" carries your curtain or draperies *around* the edge of the window casing and holds the fabric in a graceful fold down the entire window casing.

Extender-Rod Mounting, Fig. 126: Used to extend your rod to make your window look wider. This is put up on special supports attached to the window casing; the end brackets are attached to the rods and serve as the "return," but they do not touch the wall. This type of mounting will give you up to 12 inches of additional width beyond the window casing—in other words you

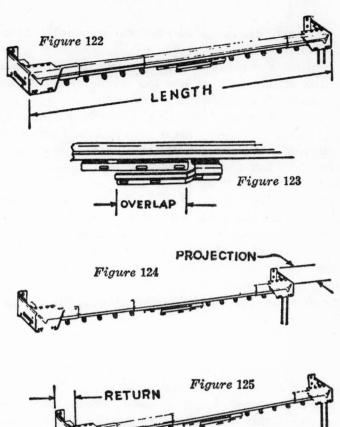

Figure 122

LENGTH

Figure 123

OVERLAP

PROJECTION

Figure 124

RETURN *Figure 125*

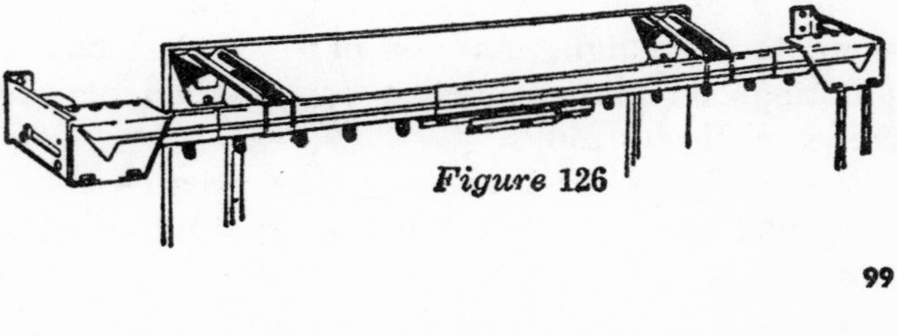

Figure 126

have apparently extended your window width as much as 24 inches!

Ceiling Mounting, Fig. 127: Needs no side brackets as it is attached directly to the ceiling. The "track" is slotted for direct mounting overhead.

Corner Window Mounting, Fig. 128: Requires two single cut-to-measure rods or two standard rods of the "one-way" draw type; install one all the way into the corner and the other one "butted" into it. Also two single traverse rods may be mounted on a single angle support in the corner. If you wish to cover the wall space in the corner, hang a stationary panel of drapery on both rods—the traverse will pull up to it.

Inside Casing Mounting, Fig. 129: Curtains that hang close to the glass are most simply handled by putting on a rod that is attached to the *inside* of the frame. Traverse rods come supplied with the necessary brackets and screws.

Casing Mounting, Fig. 130: If curtains or draperies are to cover the window but *not* to extend beyond the casing, the ordinary method of installation is to mount the brackets at the outer edges of the window casing.

Wall Mounting, Fig. 131: Used to make the window look wider, this is attached beyond the casing directly to the wall. Various types of wall construction may require plastic plugs, toggle bolts, lead plugs or screw anchors.

Plaster Screws, Fig. 132 (a): These are sufficiently strong to hold light curtains or draperies, but most mountings on plaster need a combination of plaster screws in plaster plugs.

Plastic Plugs, Fig. 132(b): Are inserted into the plaster and the screws are then inserted into the plugs.

Figure 127

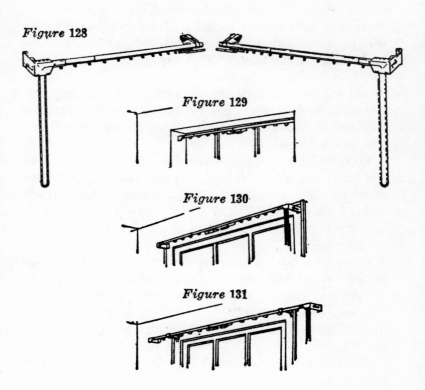

Figure 128

Figure 129

Figure 130

Figure 131

Figure 132

a   b   c   d

101

Screw Anchors, Fig. 132 (c): Many modern houses are of concrete or brick construction, and their walls require a heavier drapery installation. For neat installation mark the location of holes accurately before you start to drill holes for the screws. The screw "anchor" illustrated (sometimes called a Molly Bolt) is of lightweight metal with a slight expanding "give" to the center section of the casing. This expansion occurs when the casing is put into the wall. The screw is later inserted into this neat casing. A screw anchor holds considerable weight successfully and is widely used for "hollow" walls where an ordinary screw would pull out or become loose.

Toggle Bolts, Fig. 132 (d): Are a necessity where the walls are of wallboard or plasterboard. They are made of light metal and have a spring-action pair of "arms," which unfold back of the wall surface when inserted. "Toggles" are excellent to use if heavy draperies are involved.

Many new houses have casement windows of aluminum or steel; these require a different sort of hardware installation. If there are standard holes punched out in the steel casing you simply used a ⅜-inch No. 6 rolled thread binding head screw. Your hardware dealer carries them.

Double Traverse Rod, Fig. 133: Has two separate tracks; the inside one for glass curtains that may be ad-

Figure 133

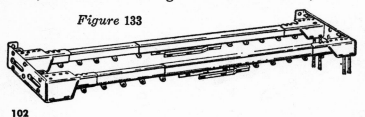

justed separately, the outside rod carries the draperies. As this is a favorite rod we give the sizes that can be obtained. Only one pair of brackets is needed.

Projection from Wall	Length in Inches
Inside rod: 1¾ to 2½ inches	30 to 48
	48 to 86
Outside rod: 4½ to 5½ inches	66 to 120
	100 to 180

Outside Traverse Rod, Fig. 134: For draperies has an inner rod that is simply a rod to hold the glass curtains. A variation of this fixture has a traverse on the inside and a plain rod on the outer bracket for holding a valance that covers the top of the draperies. Both are obtainable in a wide range of extension widths.

Double Extension Rod, Fig. 135: Is simply two rods mounted on one bracket. Use for tailored, ruffled or shirred curtains on the inside rod and a valance on the outer rod. These are rods commonly used, inexpensive, easy to install, obtainable in many sizes.

Projection from Wall	Length in Inches
1½ and 2½ inches	18 to 28
	28 to 48
	48 to 86
	66 to 120
2½ and 3½ inches	18 to 28
	28 to 48
	48 to 86
	66 to 120
3½ and 4½ inches	28 to 48
	48 to 86

Extender Rod, Fig. 136: Used to make a window seem wider and to hold a nonmovable curtain or drapery.

Adjustable Spring Tension Rod, Fig. 137: A perfect rod for use inside casings with shirred or café curtains as it has rubber-tipped ends, so no screws or nails are needed; perfect for kitchens, bathrooms, dens and playrooms. These come in 22 to 36 inches and 36 to 60 inches.

Swinging Extension Rods, Fig. 138: Are invaluable for stationary draperies and curtains that need to swing open for access to the window. Use them on dormer windows, in kitchens, bathrooms.

Length in Inches	*Projection from Wall*
15 to 24	1½ to 2½ inches

Eyelet Rodding, Fig. 139: Made of aluminum this is an easy, inexpensive way to hang curtains or draperies on odd-shaped windows, doorways or on wooden cornices as it is flexible and has extra holes to provide easy spacing of drapery or curtain hooks. It is obtainable in 5-foot lengths and is packaged to contain up to 100 feet—if you need that much!

Extender Plates, Fig. 140: To our minds, a wonder invention! Just what the home decorator needs when contending with old window frames in exasperatingly narrow widths. Do you want to make your windows look taller? Mount two extender plates on window casing, and there you are. Do you want your wooden window frames to look wider? Mount two extender plates *sideways.* Simple? Yes—and easy to do. Here are

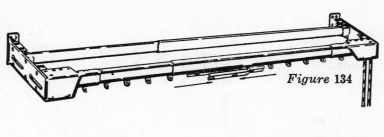

Figure 134

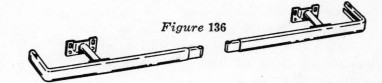

Figure 135

Figure 136

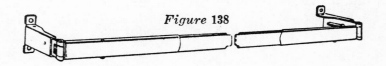

Figure 137

Figure 138

Figure 139

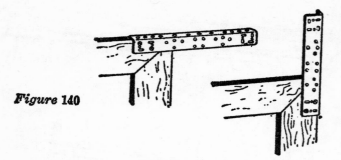

Figure 140

the sizes available: a length of 8¾ inches; 11 9/16 inches; a good long one of 18 inches.

Cord Tension Pulleys, Fig. 141: Mounted on the baseboard or floor, prevent the traverse cords from twisting, prevent searching around behind a drapery to find the cords, keep cords from dangling on the floor. They are especially useful on wide picture-window or glass-wall draperies.

One-Way Traverse Pull Fixture, Fig. 142: Needed if you are doing two windows, using just one curtain on each window. The left-hand curtain or drapery should have a *left to right* traverse pull.

Fig. 143: This figure shows the opposite, or *right to left* traverse draw. Each comes in the following measurements:

Length in Inches
32 to   50
50 to   86
86 to 150
120 to 216

Single Rod Gooseneck Brackets, Fig. 144: The simplest device to use where one needs only inexpen-

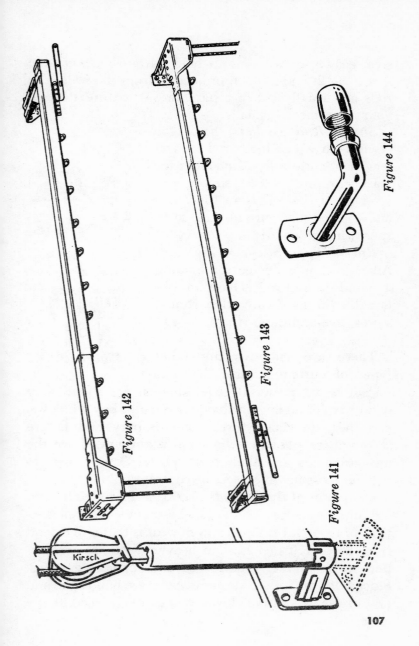

Figure 142

Figure 143

Figure 141

Figure 144

Kirsch

sive, easy-to-install rods to hold curtains. Obtainable in 1-, 1½-, 2- and 2½-inch projection from the wall. The rods are usually cut in a hardware or fixture store to your exact measurements.

Single Rod Sockets, Fig. 145: Used with a cut brass rod of any length. Wonderfully convenient for glass curtains as one simply unscrews the "barrel" from the end— and the rod and curtains are, so to speak, in the hand!

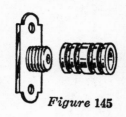

Figure 145

Barrel Type Sockets, Fig. 146: Another simple device for holding a round curtain rod. These are obtainable in hardware, department stores, five-and-dime stores.

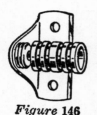

Figure 146

There are many, many other types of curtain fixtures that can be cut to your special requirements: for square bay windows, for an angular bay, for circular bay windows. For these special fixtures your drapery and fixture shop will be glad to help you. All they need are the measurements and their own special "know how" to cut the most involved sort of contraption!

Ornamental Brass Rods, Fig. 147: Intended to hold curtains, draperies or swags, these come in a permanent brass or silver finish and in widths that will extend from 28 to 150 inches. The heavier rods are for draperies, the thinner rods for curtains or café curtains. Since both the rods and the brackets are handsome and add to the decorative effect, they can be placed in any

108

Figure 147

position above the window, or across the center for café curtains.

Holdbacks, Fig. 148: These are metal rosettes that can be used with tiebacks or with ropes and tassels. There are also decorative hooks that will replace tiebacks (Fig. 149).

Cup Hooks, Fig. 150: Useful in many ways: when curtains need not be drawn across a rod but can stay in the same position, a row of cup hooks can be screwed under the top of a cornice or valance board. Small rings or drapery pins, sewed to the top of the curtains, are then fastened over these hooks. Cup hooks are fastened to the baseboard to hold the outer corners of draperies in place; they can also hold the top of the return against the window frame or cornice.

Figure 148

Figure 149

CORNICES AND VALANCE BOARDS

Properly, the word "cornice" means an architectural molding and refers chiefly to a boxed wooden frame (Fig. 151) that will cover the top of the window and conceal all the other fixtures. Metal cornices are very beautiful (Fig. 152) and can sometimes be found in antique shops or scrap-metal yards. They can also be made to order but are very costly. Wooden cornices may be carved, plain or

109

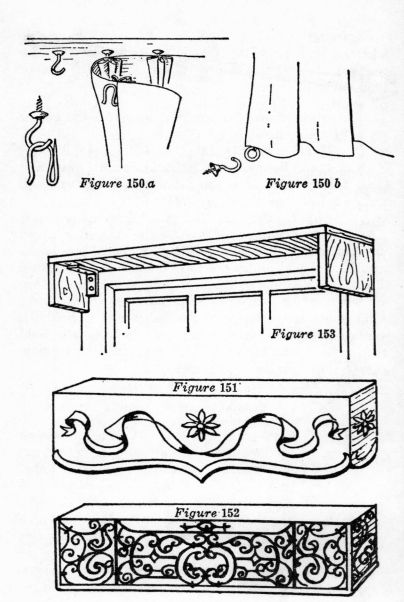

Figure 150.*a*

Figure 150 *b*

Figure 153

Figure 151

Figure 152

trimmed with strips of molding. They can be bought ready-made at some stores, or can be easily assembled by a do-it-yourself carpenter from balsa wood, plywood or wallboard. They should have a front, top and two sides. Curtain rods can be attached between the side pieces or against the wall under the cornice. Traverse tracks can be mounted under the top.

Valance boards (Fig. 153) are similar to cornices in construction. They are made of rough wood and are intended to hold fabric valances or stiffened fabric "lambrequins" that will cover them. They need only consist of a 4-inch board laid across two angle irons. If they also have end pieces, these will provide a place for attaching rods.

YARDAGES

This is a measurement chart to help you figure yardages. Add up your fabric requirements in inches, then refer to the chart to see how many yards this makes.

Inches		Yards	Inches		Yards	Inches		Yards
4½	=	⅛	126	=	3½	342	=	9½
9	=	¼	144	=	4	360	=	10
13½	=	⅜	162	=	4½	378	=	10½
18	=	½	180	=	5	396	=	11
22½	=	⅝	198	=	5½	414	=	11½
27	=	¾	216	=	6	432	=	12
31½	=	⅞	234	=	6½	450	=	12½
36	=	1	252	=	7	468	=	13
54	=	1½	270	=	7½	486	=	13½
72	=	2	288	=	8	504	=	14
90	=	2½	306	=	8½	522	=	14½
108	=	3	324	=	9	540	=	15

Inches		Yards	Inches		Yards	Inches		Yards
558	=	15½	684	=	19	810	=	22½
576	=	16	702	=	19½	828	=	23
594	=	16½	720	=	20	846	=	23½
612	=	17	738	=	20½	864	=	24
630	=	17½	756	=	21	882	=	24½
648	=	18	774	=	21½	900	=	25
666	=	18½	792	=	22			

Measure from the rod or from the base of the ring for the finished length. Curtains may end at the window sill, at the base of the apron (Fig. 154) or at the floor. Draperies always end at the floor; some formal draperies may even sweep the floor (Fig. 155). If carpeting extends to the windows, the curtains should clear them.

Curtains or draperies that are to be looped back may have to be cut longer at the center edges than at the sides. After they have been looped back, the inner (draped) edges should be about 12 inches shorter than the straight edges (Fig. 156). Use a string to determine how long the draped edge should be; attach it to the rod, draw it over the spot where the tie-back will be, leaving enough free to drape gracefully, then let it fall to within 12 inches of where the curtain will end (Fig. 157). If this measurement is longer than the outer, or straight, edge of curtain, cut the fabric diagonally, allowing for the bottom hem, which will be slanted.

Decide on the finished length from top to bottom. Remember that the curtain may start slightly above the rod to hide it when planning pinch pleats or other pleated top finishes.

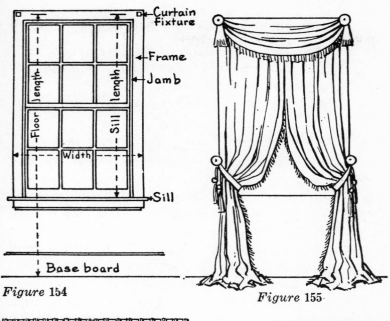

Figure 154

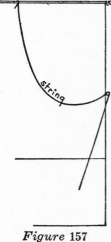

Figure 155

Figure 156

Figure 157

113

Add the amount needed for hems:

Sheer fabrics need double hems, so add 6 inches.
Unlined curtains of non-sheer fabric need single 3-inch hems, so add 3½ inches.
Draperies need 5-inch hems, so add 5½ inches.

Now add the amount needed for finishing the top:

Casing and heading require 3½ inches above the rod.

Pinch pleats, box pleats, cartridge pleats need 1 inch if you are using ready-made tape, 10 inches if you are using buckram or pellon.

Shirring requires 1 inch if you are using shirring-tape, 3½ inches if you are making casings for cords.

Scallops will take 1 inch, *plus* the depth of the scallops.

Lined draperies need only ½ inch for top finishing.

After you have determined the exact length needed for the hem and the top finishing, decide how many lengths you need to make the curtains the correct width. Remember that you will have to make each pair of curtains from two to three times the width of the rod. Lined draperies should be from two to two and one-half times this width, sheer curtains three times this width. On figured fabrics, pattern must match on all the curtains, so allow one repeat of the design for each additional length. Often one and one-half widths are sufficient for one curtain; in this case, *the seam should be near the side of the window. When joining widths, be sure to make a left-hand and a right-hand curtain for each window.* If the rod has a return (the distance away from the wall), add this measurement to the width. Allow for the seams, removing selvage, and for side hems. Sheer fabrics should have double side hems, so allow 8 inches for the two side hems; other fabrics will need 5 inches for both side hems.

If you plan to use ready-made pleating tape, buy the tape and the hooks first. Insert the hooks in the tape until the tape is the correct width for half the rod, plus any return and any overlap. Be sure to use end pins in the end pockets. When the tape has pockets spaced about 1¼ inches apart, use four pockets for the pinch-pleat hooks, then skip a pocket; for greater fullness, use all the pockets. If the tape has the pockets close together, the pleats can be deeper by skipping two or three pockets between the prongs of the pinch-pleat hooks. For making box pleats or cartridge pleats, use only two of the four prongs and space them any distance for the effect you prefer. When the tape has been gathered to the desired width, cut the tape, allowing ½ inch at each end for finishing, remove the hooks and measure the length of the tape. This will be the finished width of each curtain. Figs. 158, 159 and 160 show the three kinds of ready-made tape for use with pinch-pleat hooks.

Lined draperies are usually cut 6 inches longer than finished length.

Drapery linings are cut 3 inches shorter and 4 inches narrower than the drapery fabric.

Be sure to include any fabric needed for valances,

Figure 158

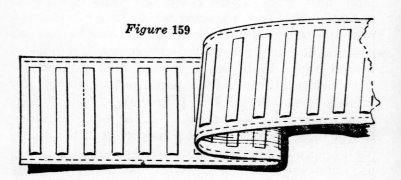

Figure 159

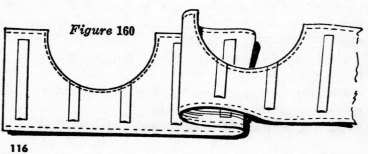

Figure 160

tiebacks or ruffles. Yardage for ruffles is given with ruffled curtains.

Another consideration when planning the width of a curtain or drapery is the "bunched" width when they are drawn aside. This will usually be one-third of the total width, depending on the weight of the fabric and whether it is lined. This is one of the reasons why heavy fabric and lined draperies may have less fullness than sheer fabrics without looking skimpy.

Finally, be sure to allow a little extra fabric for cutting the lengths; the ends may be uneven and need straightening, and you may want to allow an extra inch on each length in case there should be any fraying.

GLASS-CURTAIN FABRICS

Glass curtains are primarily for screening out the light and should be subordinated to the draperies in order not to detract from the decorative effect of the room. "Thin and shadowy" is the keynote when selecting fabric to put directly against window glass. To insure obtaining the exact effect you want, always hold a sample of the material to the sunlight to test its light-filtering property.

China Silk: A material greatly used in the past but not so easily found today as the synthetics are available in such wide ranges of price and color.

Gauze (Silk): It is one of the best to use because of its thin translucent quality. When glass curtains are made one or two shades lighter than the color of the walls, the effect is most pleasing. If using gauze full length to the floor, a charming decorator effect is obtained if two tones are used—one for the window curtains, a slightly darker shade for overdraperies. For windows on stairways, for French doors, for small problem windows such as the high-up, small windows seen at either side of a fireplace in older houses, the best treatment is to dim them down by using a wall-toned gauze simply shirred at top and bottom and attached to windows by means of small firm rods. In this treatment be sure your bottom rod takes up the "stretch" of the curtain and maintains a proper taut-ness. Silk gauze is obtainable in wide ranges of color from white to pastels, to darks and very darks. For modern ranch-type houses, the beiges, cocoas, oyster whites are greatly favored.

Ninon: This is a cellulose acetate rayon having a silky, flat and smooth effect. It comes in a very wide range of colors: white, ecru, beiges, yellow, shrimp, greens, coppers—a gamut from pale shades to deep. It may also be used without overdrapes if economy is a requirement or a desirability.

Nylon, Orlon and Dynel: Splendid for glass curtains as they are dirt and moisture resistant, easily washed, usually drip-dried or dripped to the point where they can be put back on the rods and allowed to dry there.

Organdy: This is a favorite material for window curtains as it is a sheer cotton, thin and very crisp in feeling. When purchasing, it is advisable always to ask for the "permanent-finish" type so that it can be laundered innumerable times and still retain the built-in finish. This material, unlike the softer finishes, drapes beautifully and is entirely satisfactory to use without overdrapes as it bends and rounds the corners at the sides of the windows. It is most happily combined with chintz draperies in semiformal living rooms. For decades it has been beloved in bedrooms as its most outstanding characteristic is one of gay femininity, lightness, grace. One might almost call it a "light-hearted" material. The best methods of treating organdy are fluting, ruffling, pleating, draping. Tie it back at window sills—it delights in being pretty! Color ranges are wide, and there are very attractive "shadow" organdies and embroidered Swiss organdies. The latter are apt to be a bit on the expensive side as many of them are imported.

Scrim: One of the most popular, inexpensive and easy-to-handle fabrics ever invented. It hems well, falls well, has sufficient loose-weave body to look trim, hangs best when undraped. The most satisfactory method of using is simply to hang it on a rod or make a heading or small grouped pleats. Comes in white, ecru, cream color.

Swiss Muslin: A fine opaque cotton available in plain colors, or with woven dots in white or colors. Charming in bedrooms, bathrooms, breakfast rooms, on dressing tables. Makes a perfect tieback curtain as it drapes easily and gracefully. Match it up with summer bedspreads for a "cool" look.

Voile: A more finely woven material than scrim, it is obtainable in many colors—orchid, yellows, greens, blues, pinks, as well as white. It also is best handled by a simple shirring treatment on a top rod or in a series of small pinch-pleats. As it is rather limp in texture, it does not drape or tie back as successfully as does organdy.

UNLINED CURTAINS

The selvage must be removed from all material, or fabric will pucker. When cutting curtains, straighten the end of the fabric by drawing a thread. If the weave prevents this, or if fabric is badly slanted and cannot be straightened, fold the fabric across the width with the selvages even on both sides (Fig. 161), then cut along this fold. Cut each length in the same way, taking care to match any patterns exactly. The patterns should match not only on one curtain but on every pair.

Join the widths with narrow French seams (Fig. 162), or narrow felled seams (Fig. 163). If stitching on the machine, be sure to adjust the tension and the length of the stitch so that the seams do not pull. The adjustments will depend on the fabric, so it is best to try out the stitching on a scrap piece (see needle and thread chart on page 243).

Next, make the side hems. These should be about 2 inches wide and look best if sewed by hand using blind stitches (Fig. 164). On sheer fabrics all hems should be double (Fig. 165). On other fabrics, turn back ½ inch on wrong side and stitch, then fold a 2-inch hem (Fig. 166). The bottom hem can be left until last; when the curtain has been tried on the rod, measure the length and mark it before sewing. Weighted tape (Fig. 167) can be inserted in the hem to hold the curtain in even folds and to improve the appearance.

The top of the curtain can now be finished in one of the following ways:

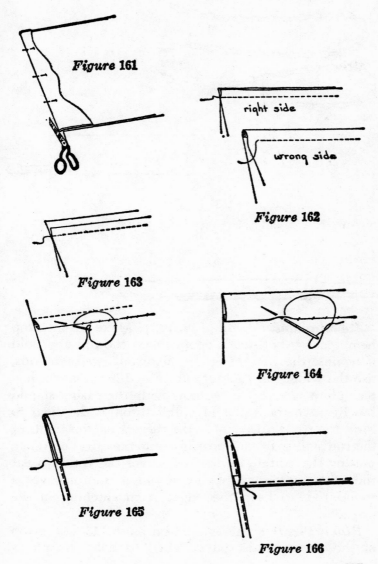

Figure 161

right side

wrong side

Figure 162

Figure 163

Figure 164

Figure 165

Figure 166

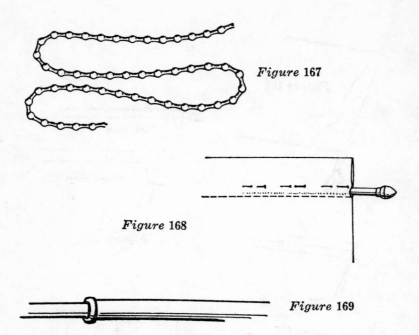

Figure 167

Figure 168

Figure 169

Heading and Casing (Fig. 168): Make a 3-inch top hem, leaving both ends open. Insert the rod and hold it against the bottom of the hem; on extension rods, use the wider part of the rod (Fig. 169). Place a few pins above the rod to see how wide the casing should be. Remove the rod and stitch through the hem to form the casing. Do not make the casing too tight, or the rod will snag and possibly tear the curtain. When putting the curtain on the rod, cover the end of a flat rod with a piece of paper, or put a thimble over a round rod, to keep the edges from catching in the material.

Pinch Pleats (see Fig. 157 on page 113): The top of the curtain must be stiffened to hold the pleats

122

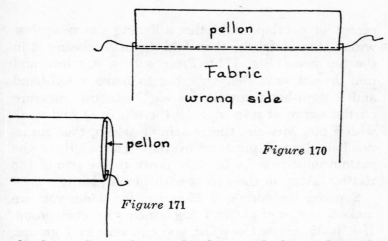

pellon

Fabric

wrong side

pellon

Figure 170

Figure 171

firmly in place. This can be done with the ready-made tape, or with buckram or pellon.

If the tape has been measured in advance and the curtain hemmed to the correct width, as explained in the section on yardage, cut all tapes to the same width and number of pockets. If the rod has a return, remember to make a left-hand and a right-hand curtain for each window, or groups of windows. Turn down 1 inch of top on wrong side, then pin tape to curtain, covering raw edge of fabric and turning under the ends of tape. Stitch across top, sides and bottom of tape, or stitch across the top and stitch the bottom only where the pinch pleats will hide the stitching. Insert the pins, hang the curtain, then mark and hem bottom edge.

If you wish to use buckram or pellon and hand-made pleats, you will need a strip of stiffening about 4 inches wide and as long as top of curtain. Place this strip on the wrong side of fabric with the edges overlapping ½ inch (Fig. 170). Stitch them together at center of overlap. Fold the stiffening down against wrong side of fabric, then fold again, enclosing it in the top hem (Fig. 171). Press with a dry iron and pin; do not sew. Remembering to make a left-hand and a right-hand curtain for each window, measure off the return at side edge (if there is one) and mark with a pin. Measure the remaining width, then measure half the rod plus any overlap. The width of the curtain must now be brought down to the size of the rod by taking in the excess with pinch pleats.

Suppose the curtain is 25 inches too wide; you can make 5 groups of pleats, using 5 inches for each group. If it is 35 inches too wide, you can take in 7 groups, using 5 inches for each group. Always plan an uneven number of groups because it is easier to space them if there is one group at center. Mark position of first pleat about 3 inches beyond the return, mark last pleat about 3 inches from center overlap or center edge. Fold the curtain in half with these two markers meeting and mark center fold. Divide each side into equal spaces and mark. Pin a large pleat at each marker (Fig. 172), taking in 5 inches, or the necessary amount, for each pleat.

When all the pleats have been pinned in place,

Figure 172

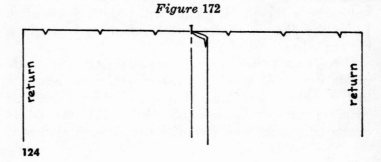

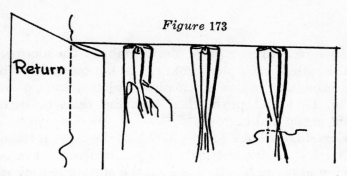

Figure 173

Return

measure the curtain against the rod to check the width. Adjust the pins, if necessary, to make the pleats deeper or shallower. When the pleats are pinned satisfactorily, stitch each pleat from top to bottom of hem. Take the center fold of the pleat and push it back against the stitching line (see Fig. 173), forming each large pleat into three pinch pleats. Stitch these three pleats in place across the bottom, just below edge of stiffening. The pleats may be left free at the top to fan out, or may be blind-stitched together at the top. Use drapery pins for hanging curtain.

Box Pleats: As in the case of pinch pleats, the top of the curtain needs stiffening. You can use the pleater tape and pins, as described in the section on yardage, or the top hem can be reinforced with buckram or pellon. Either of these is applied in the same way as for pinch pleats.

For handmade box pleats, measure off any return at the side edge and any overlap at center edge and mark. Starting about 3 inches beyond these markers, fold curtain to make a pleat about 2 inches deep. Skip about 5 inches, then make another pleat the same depth. Continue across in this way, having pleats evenly spaced. Try curtain against window rod to check the width and adjust the pins to make pleats deeper or narrower until the curtain is the desired width. Stitch each pleat from top to bottom of hem in the same way as for pinch pleats. Flatten each pleat (Fig. 174) and press, then tack the sides of each pleat at top and bottom.

Cartridge Pleats (Fig. 175): Use the same method as for box pleats, but make the pleats about 2 inches deep and closer together. Adjust the curtain to desired width, then stitch each pleat from top to bottom of hem. Insert a roll of buckram or pellon in each pleat and tack in place by hand. Use drapery pins for hanging curtain.

Shirring: There is a ready-made shirring tape (Fig. 176) with four woven-in cords, that will simplify your work. Before using this tape, draw the cords from the tape about 1½ inches from the ends and knot them. This will keep them from pulling out when cords are drawn up. Fold under the end of the tape beyond the cords for a neat edge. Turn 1 inch of curtain to wrong side and pin tape over this raw edge. Stitch top edge of tape in place, cut tape 1 inch beyond edge of curtain; remove cords from this seam allowance, knot ends and turn under raw edge of tape. Stitch tape across both ends and lower edge. Draw up cords to desired length and tie ends together at the outer edge of curtain. These cords can be released for laundering, or cut off. If the cords are cut, stitch the rows of gathers in place.

If you do not use the shirring tape, turn back ½ inch at top of curtain, then fold a 3-inch hem. Stitch hem, then make a heading by stitching 1 inch from top. Make rows of stitching ½ inch apart across bottom of hem, dividing it into ½-inch casings. Run cords or tape

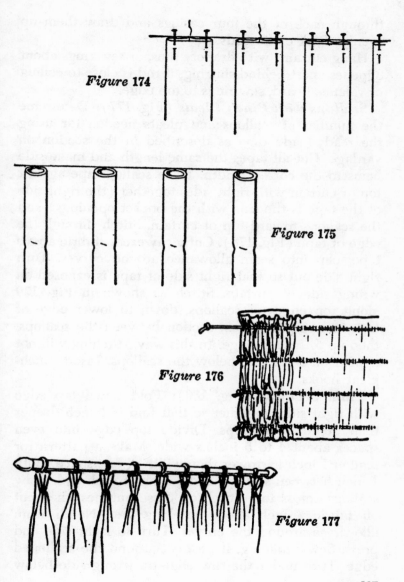

Figure 174

Figure 175

Figure 176

Figure 177

through each of the four casings and draw them up evenly. Tack or tie ends.

Hang curtains with drapery pins, or sew rings about 3 inches apart behind shirring; if rod is close to ceiling or valance board, sew rings to top edge.

Scallops with Pinch Pleats (Fig. 177): Determine the number of scallops and pleats needed for using the ready-made tape as described in the section on yardage. Cut all tapes the same length and make side hems to the correct width. Place scallop tape against top of curtain with right sides together (the right side of the tape is the side with the pocket openings) and the scallops toward top of curtain. Stitch through the edge of tape (Fig. 178). Cut away excess fabric above tape, clip into seam allowance around curves. Turn right side out so that right side of tape is exposed on wrong side of curtain. Stitch as shown in Fig. 179 along top edges of scallops, down to lower edge of tape, across pinch-pleat section between the scallops, then up to scallop edge. In this way, stitching will not appear on right side below the scallops. Insert pinch-pleat hooks.

Plain Scallops (Fig. 180): Fold down top edge with right sides together so that fold is 1 inch deeper than depth of scallops. Divide top edge into even spaces about 4 to 5 inches wide. Make a pattern for scallop 1 inch narrower than width of one space. With 1 inch between scallops and 1 inch at each end, draw scallops across top. Stitch on these outlines, then cut off fabric ½ inch above stitching line. Notch seam allowance around the curves. Turn to right side and press. Sew trimming, if desired, around the scalloped edge. Turn under the raw edge on wrong side below

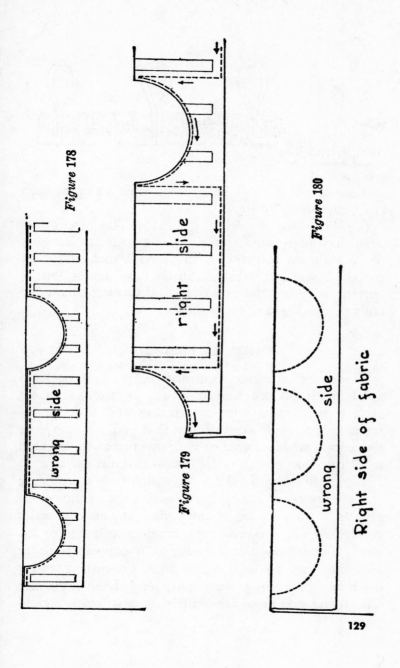

Figure 178

Figure 179

Figure 180

wrong side

right side

wrong side

Right side of fabric

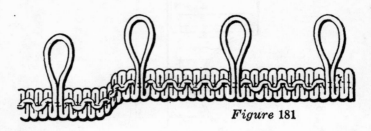

Figure 181

scallops and hem in place by hand. Sew a ring to each
tab between scallops.

Café Curtain Braid (Fig. 181): This decorative
braid has loops woven in along one edge for hanging
the curtain on the rod. Turn down 1 inch at top of
curtain toward right side. Stitch tape across top of
curtain, covering the raw edge and turning under the
ends of the braid at each end.

SHEETS AS CURTAINS

There are so many beautiful colors and patterns
available in sheets, that they can be used to make
attractive curtains with no cutting and little or no
sewing. If there is a possibility that you may move or
redecorate within a year or two, sheets make a sensible
substitute for curtains. Whereas curtains seldom fit
any windows besides those for which they were made
and are therefore a complete loss elsewhere, sheets can
always be put into use on the beds. They are especially
good for college dormitories, summer cottages or for
newly married couples in their first apartment. In order
that they can be used again later, no cutting and a
minimum of sewing are recommended. Selvages are
left on and side hems are omitted. Any stitching should

be done loosely enough so that it can be ripped without damaging the sheets.

Sheet Sizes: Plan to buy sheets that will fit your beds. Although only flat sheets will make curtains, you will be able to supplement these later with fitted sheets and pillow cases. As a convenience, we include all of these in the following list of sizes.

Flat Sheets

Twin	72 x 108 inches
Long Twin	72 x 117½ inches
Extra-Long Twin	72 x 120 inches
Double	81 x 108 inches
Long Double	81 x 117½ inches
Extra-Long Double	81 x 120 inches
Large Double	90 x 108 inches
King Size	108 x 122½ inches
Cot Size	54 x 99 inches

Bottom Fitted Sheets	*For Mattress Size*
Twin 57 x 94 inches	39 x 75 inches
Twin Foam Rubber 57 x 93 inches	39 x 75 inches
Double 72 x 94 inches	54 x 75 inches
Double Foam Rubber 72 x 92 inches	54 x 75 inches
Long Twin 57 x 98 inches	39 x 80 inches
Long Double 72 x 98 inches	54 x 80 inches
Queen Size 78 x 98 inches	60 x 80 inches

	Top Fitted Sheets	Regular Pillow Cases
Twin	72 x 101 inches	42 x 38½ inches
Double	81 x 101 inches	45 x 38½ inches

Special Pillow Cases

Foam Rubber	38 x 36 inches
Bolster	42 x 48 inches

In Fig. 182 a pair of flowered sheets has been mounted on shirring tape and attached to the rod with rings. They have been shortened with tucks; ball fringe is sewed to each tuck and repeated across the top.

Fig. 183 shows a pair of sheets with coin dots. They have been outlined with moss fringe in a co-ordinated color, then mounted on pinch-pleat tape. The extra length has been taken up in a top and bottom hem.

Another suggestion is shown in Fig. 184 where the tops of the sheets are turned down to form a valance and fastened to the rod with clip rings or clip hooks. Do not use drapery pins, as they would mar the fabric. The pastel color of the sheets is accentuated with cotton-tufted tape along the edge of the valance and around the curtains.

LINED DRAPERIES

The purpose of lining draperies is fourfold: it gives a richer appearance by keeping the light from filtering through one thickness of fabric; it protects the fabric from sunlight and dust; it adds weight so that the

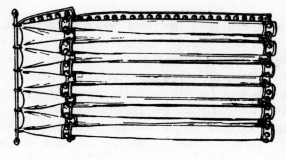

Figure 184

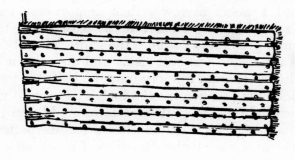

Figure 183

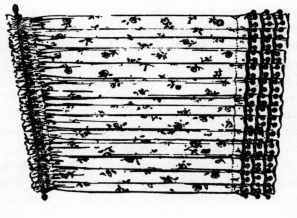

Figure 182

133

drapery will fall in softer and more graceful folds; and it gives a uniform appearance from the street.

Cream-colored or white sateen is the approved material for linings, although unbleached muslin or any similar goods can be substituted, *provided the lining is of lighter weight than the curtain material.*

Yardage: Decide on the finished length (see yardage information at the beginning of this section). Each length of the drapery material is cut 6 inches longer than finished length; lining is cut 3 inches shorter and 4 inches narrower than drapery material. Each pair of draperies should be *at least* twice the width of rod, preferably 2½ times the width, plus about 12 inches for seams and side hems and any return or overlap. Each separate drapery must be helf this total width; each lining section is cut 4 inches narrower than the drapery fabric. For patterned fabric, add one repeat of the design for each additional length; pattern should match across all the draperies. *Cut off all selvages.*

Straighten edge and cut lengths in the same way as for unlined curtains. Matching any patterns, join widths of fabric. If the seam is off center, remember that it should fall toward the side of the window and that there must be a left-hand and a right-hand drapery for each window. Join widths of lining so that the seams will meet the seams on the draperies wherever possible.

Turn up ½ inch to wrong side at bottom of drapery and stitch, then turn up a 5-inch hem. Sew hem by hand. Turn up ½ inch at lower edge of lining on wrong side, then turn up 2-inch hem and stitch this hem. Place drapery and lining with right sides together and hem of lining covering 2 inches of drapery hem (Fig. 185). Check to see that lining is 4 inches narrower than drapery. Pin side edges together, making sure that hems are the same distance apart on both sides. Place on the sewing machine *with lining on top.* Stitch both sides ½ inch from edge; one seam will be stitched from top to bottom, the other seam from bottom to top (Fig. 186).

Lay the drapery on a flat surface and smooth the lining evenly so that 2 inches of drapery extend beyond lining on both sides for hems. Baste top edges together. Measure from drapery hem to top for finished length and mark this length on the lining with pencil, straight across the top. Cut a piece of buckram 4 inches wide and same length as width of drapery. Place this strip below pencil line and just covering it. Stitch through all three thicknesses on pencil line, keeping fabric taut (Fig. 187). Turn drapery right side out. Press entire drapery. Make pinch pleats, box pleats or cartridge pleats as described for unlined curtains (see pages 122–126). Fasten bottom hem of lining to hem of drapery with three or four French tacks (Fig. 188). Hang draperies with drapery pins and fasten outer corners to baseboard with small rings sewed to draperies and cup hooks attached to baseboard. Any top return should also be fastened in place.

CURTAINS ON TOP AND BOTTOM RODS

A rod at top and bottom will hold glass curtains tightly in place on French doors (Fig. 189) or window panes (Fig. 190) so that they will not swing out when doors or windows are opened. They should be mounted on thin brass rods (see fixtures on page 108), fastened

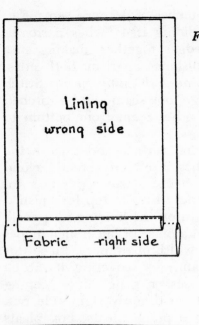

Figure 185

Lining
wrong side

Fabric   right side

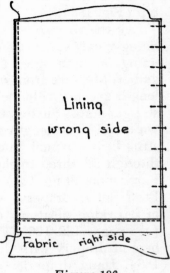

Lining
wrong side

Fabric   right side

Figure 186

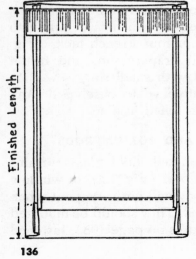

Finished Length

Figure 187

136

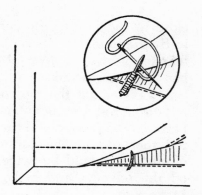

Figure 188

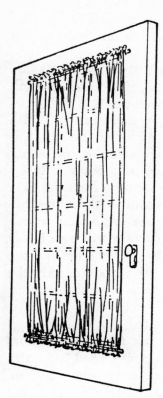

Figure 189

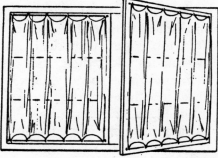

Figure 190

close to the frames. Be sure the rods are rust proof so that curtains can be replaced while still damp after laundering. Use a sheer fabric with a firm weave, that has been preshrunk.

Always mount the top rod first, then mark position of bottom rod, but *do not attach it*. Measure the length between the top rod and the desired position of bottom rod, then add 8 inches for headings and casings. Width of curtains should be twice the width of the rod. Cut off the selvages and make 1-inch double side hems. Make 2-inch double hems at top and bottom. Insert one rod in top hem to determine width of casing, then stitch across both hems to form casings. Mount curtain on top rod, insert free rod in bottom casing and attach the fixtures for this rod so that curtain will be slightly stretched and taut. Make all the other curtains the same length and mount all the other rods exactly the same distance apart, so that curtains will be interchangeable.

To make café curtains mounted on two rods as shown in Fig. 191, use preshrunk fabric and lining twice the width of rods. If rings are used, no extra seam allowance will be needed at top and bottom. Cut off selvages and join widths of fabric and lining to desired width of curtain. Press seams. Place fabric and lining with right sides together and baste edges. Fold top edge to divide it into equal spaces about 4 to 6 inches wide, then draw zigzags or scallops, fitting them into these spaces. Mark lower edge to correspond. Stitch on these marked lines, then stitch sides ½ inch from edges, leaving a space on one side for turning curtain right side out. Cut off seam allowance ½ inch beyond shaped stitching lines, clip into corners between zigzags or notch curves of scallops. Turn curtain to right side and press. Sew opening. Sew on any decorative tape or fringe; sew on rings. Mount curtain on top rod, insert other rod through bottom rings and attach fixtures for this rod so that curtain will be taut. Make all curtains exactly the same length and mount other rods exactly the same distance apart so that curtains will be interchangeable.

FANLIGHT CURTAINS

A curtain to fit a fanlight properly (Fig. 192) is a job for a professional and too difficult for an amateur. It should be mounted on a curved rod that has been custom-made for the curve of the fanlight.

RUFFLED CURTAINS

Cut strips for ruffles on length of goods to avoid extra seams. Ruffles may be from 2 to about 6 inches wide, depending on the amount of body in the material. Crisp fabric can be used for wide ruffles, but soft material will look better with narrow ruffles. The wider the ruffle, the more fullness is needed; narrow ruffles can be twice the finished length, wide ruffles need triple fullness.

The edges of the curtain that are to be trimmed with ruffles need only narrow hems for ruffles with headings (Fig. 193), and are left unfinished if ruffles have no headings. Measure the edges that are to be trimmed with ruffles, then multiply this length by two, two and one-half or three, depending on the amount of fullness required. For a ruffle with a heading, add 1 inch to

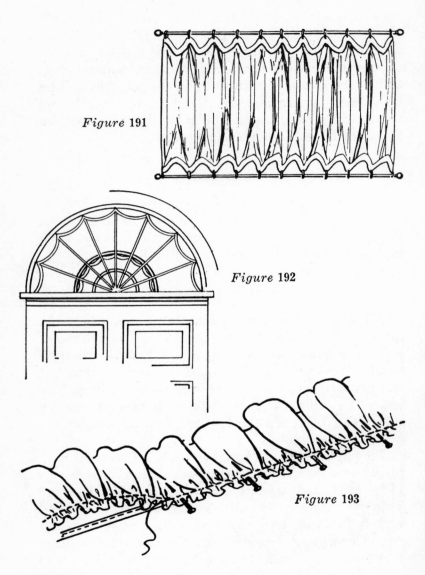

Figure 191

Figure 192

Figure 193

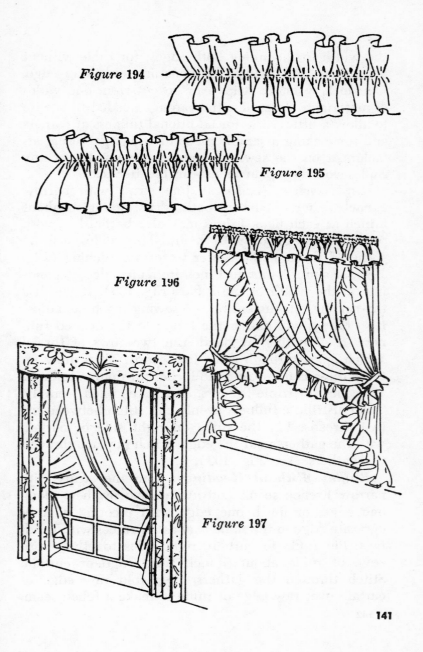

Figure 194

Figure 195

Figure 196

Figure 197

the width for hemming both edges; for ruffle without a heading, add ½ inch for hemming only one edge. Decide how many strips can be cut from one width of material to determine the yardage needed. It is wise to allow a little extra, for additional fullness at corners and for making a sample piece to adjust gathering attachment on the sewing machine. Do not forget any ruffles you may plan to use on the tiebacks.

Ruffles with Headings: Join strips with narrow French seams, then hem both edges, taking in about ½ inch at each hem. Edges may also be finished with picoting instead of with hems. The ruffles can be gathered through the center to form a ruching (Fig. 194), or about ½ inch to 1 inch from one edge, depending on the width of the ruffle (Fig. 195). If you use the ruffling attachment on the sewing machine, adjust it so that it will gather the fabric to the desired fullness. If gathering by hand, run two rows of thread ¼ inch apart through ruffle for 1 yard. Then draw up these threads to measure 18 inches for double fullness, 12 inches for triple fullness, and fasten ends securely. Then distribute fullness evenly and stitch between the two threads. Pin the ruffle on right side of curtain with the gathers near the edge. Stitch in place through the gathers (see Fig. 193).

Ruffles Without Headings: Join the strips with narrow French seams and make a narrow hem along one edge, or finish one edge with picoting. Gather opposite edge in the same way as for ruffles with headings. Pin ruffle to curtain, right sides together, with edge of ruffle about ¼ inch from edge of curtain. Stitch through the gathers, then fold raw edge of curtain over raw edge of ruffle to make a felled seam.

Sew this seam by hand or stitch it on the machine (see Fig. 163 on page 121).

CRISSCROSS CURTAINS

Made of sheer fabric, each curtain should cover at least three-fourths of the window area and be made about two and one-half times the width of this measurement. If the curtains overlap the entire window (Fig. 196), so that they cover all of the rod, they will need no valance but can be finished with a top ruffle. However, if they overlap only part way and the rod is exposed, the tops should be covered with a valance. To mount crisscross curtains on one rod, they can be overlapped and sewed together before the top edges are finished, then the heading and casing made with the double thickness.

Most crisscross curtains are made of organdy, dotted swiss or similar material and trimmed with ruffles. They can also be made for formal rooms: make them of silk taffeta and trim them with fringe or looped braid or leave them untrimmed. This type of crisscross curtain can be used under draperies or with lambrequins (Fig. 197).

Yardage: See Fig. 156 on page 113 for planning the extra length of the draped edges. To this length add 6 inches for a double hem and 3 inches for heading and casing. If planning ruffles, be sure to include enough fabric for making these and follow the instructions for ruffled curtains. Allow also for ruffled tiebacks.

Cut off all selvages and join widths with narrow French seams. If no ruffles are to be added, make

2-inch double side hems. Make a 3-inch double hem at lower edge. Remember that this hem will slant between the draped measurement at inner edge and the straight measurement at outer edge, and that there must be a left-hand and a right-hand curtain for each window. Each curtain may have a separate casing and heading, or the pair may be overlapped to make one casing and heading to fit on one rod. If they are overlapped, be sure to overlap them correctly: when there are two windows, the curtain closest to the corner of the room should be on the outside (Fig. 198).

To gather the curtains properly so that they will drape in the most graceful folds at all times, shirring tape can be stitched diagonally across the curtain on the wrong side (Fig. 199). Hang the curtains on the rods and mark the outer edges where tiebacks or holdbacks will be placed. Take the center edge and drape it toward the tieback marker so that it curves softly.

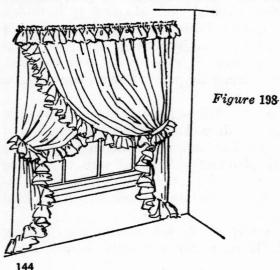

Figure 198

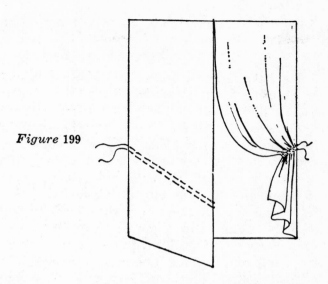

Figure 199

Mark this point at center edge. Remove curtains from rods and draw a diagonal line between markers, making sure that these lines correspond exactly on both curtains. Cut two-cord shirring tape about 3 inches longer than this line. Remove cords from the tape for 1½ inches at each end and knot them securely. Fold under the raw ends of tape beyond the knots and stitch tape in place along both edges. Draw up cords from side edge of curtain to desired length and tie. Cords may be released for laundering. Plain 1-inch tape can also be used; stitch it in place at both long edges and at center, forming two channels. Cut a piece of cord twice the length of tape plus about 4 inches. Starting at draped edge, run one end of cord through one channel, other end through other channel. Draw up cord and tie both ends together, distributing fullness evenly.

TIEBACKS

Tiebacks can be of several different types and should be suitable for the curtains or draperies with which they will be used.

Tailored Tiebacks (Fig. 200): These are suitable for plain curtains and should be wide enough and firm enough so that they will not look stringy. They can be from 2 to 4 inches wide and as long as necessary to drape the curtains into the desired position. Crisp fabric can be cut four times the finished width. Fold in half, right sides together, then fold each edge toward center (Fig. 201). Stitch both ends, then turn right side out, forming a band of four thicknesses. Sew edges together. Trim with fringe, braid or contrasting fabric to match valance. If fabric is soft, it should be lined with crinoline, buckram or pellon. Cut the stiffening the width of finished tiebacks; cut fabric twice this width plus 1 inch. Place stiffening on wrong side of fabric and turn ½ inch over it (Fig. 202). Turn back ½ inch at opposite edge of fabric, then fold fabric in half over the stiffening and sew edges together. Turn under raw ends and sew.

Ruffled Tiebacks: These are correct for ruffled curtains. The length can be from 12 inches to 24 inches, depending on the amount of fullness they are to hold in place. If diagonal shirring has been used, make tiebacks twice this length. On a ruffled curtain the tiebacks need not cover the ruffles but can be slipped through an opening between the curtain and the ruffle. The band can be about 2 inches wide. If the fabric is soft, cut the band four times this width,

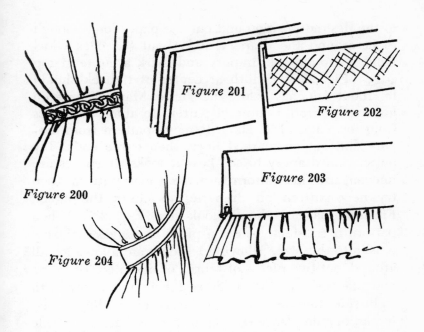

Figure 201

Figure 202

Figure 203

Figure 200

Figure 204

then fold raw edges to meet at center. Fold in half, enclosing the raw edges. If the ruffle has no heading, insert raw edge of ruffle between the two folds (Fig. 203), turn under ends of band and stitch. If ruffle has a heading, turn under ends of band, then stitch edges together. Stitch ruffle in place. For a tieback with ruffles on both edges, cut two bands, each twice the finished width. Fold edges to meet at center, then place bands together with ruffles between the folds. Turn under ends of bands and stitch.

Drapery Tiebacks (Fig. 204): These can match the draperies or the valance. They should be shaped and stiffened with canvas. Make a pattern with wrapping paper. Decide on the length that will hold the fullness to the desired position and cut the paper long enough to fit around the drapery and about 8 inches wide. Hold it around the drapery and mark a curve at top edge (Fig. 205). Width at center of tieback should be about 4 inches below this curve. Mark a curve on lower edge from bottom of pattern to about 2½ inches from top edge (Fig. 206). Remove pattern from drapery and cut on marked lines, then curve ends. Try pattern on drapery to see how it looks. If curves are uneven, use this pattern to make a new pattern, then try new pattern on draperies to check the effect. Finished pattern should look like Fig. 207. When pattern is satisfactory, cut a piece of canvas or heavy muslin to this size. Allowing ½ inch seam allowance all around, cut two pieces of fabric, or one piece of fabric and one piece of lining. Place fabric and lining with right sides together, canvas centered over lining. Leaving an opening large enough to turn tieback right side out, stitch close to edge of canvas (Fig. 208). Clip seam allowance, turn tieback right side out and slip-stitch opening together.

Cords and Tassels: These can be bought ready-made in both cotton and rayon and come in a variety of colors. Two loops of cord are fastened together with a tassel. If you wish, you can assemble your own.

Attaching Tiebacks: Fabric tiebacks can be equipped with small plastic rings at each end. These are then held in place by a cup hook fastened to the side of the window. If you have decorative holdbacks (illustrated on page 109) the ends of the tiebacks or the cords can be looped over them. Wing-shaped holdbacks can replace tiebacks.

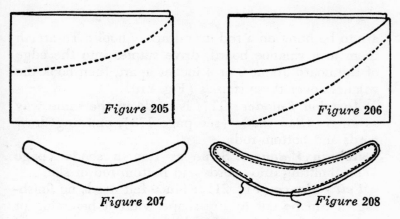

Figure 205

Figure 206

Figure 207

Figure 208

VALANCES

A valance is any top covering for the window made of unstiffened fabric. It can be made to hang from a rod or from a valance board. All valances are intended to complete the window decoration and to conceal the rods or any other fixtures. They should be deep enough to hide these fixtures; if made too deep they will make the window and curtains appear shorter and the ceiling lower. This is desirable only if the windows are very tall and narrow or the ceiling too high. Many of the following valances are made in the same way as curtains.

Ruffled Valance with Casing: This is meant to hang from a rod and is finished in the same way as a curtain with heading and casing. For sheer ruffled curtains, they are trimmed with ruffles to match the curtains. Made of calico or chintz, this type of valance can also be combined with café curtains or with shutters (Fig. 209).

Pinch-Pleated, Box-Pleated and Cartridge-Pleated Valances: Made in the same way as curtains. If they

149

are to be hung on a rod, use drapery hooks. To attach them to a valance board, drive staples into the edge of the board about 3 or 4 inches apart, then hook the valances over these staples (Fig. 210).

Austrian Valance: This is made in the same way as an Austrian shade (see page 173), omitting draw cords and bottom rod.

Roman Valance: Same as Roman shade (page 171), omitting draw cords and bottom rod or slat.

Felt Valance (Fig. 211): Since felt needs no finishing, it can be cut to any shape without hemming or lining. To hang it on a rod, sew a casing of carpet binding under the top edge, cupping the casing slightly to allow for the thickness of the rod (Fig. 212). To attach it to a valance board, stitch a piece of tape under the top edge, leaving lower edge of tape free. Drive tacks through the tape under the valance (Fig. 213). It can also be attached to the valance board with decorative brass upholstery nails evenly spaced across. Draw a chalk line for the row of nails, then mark even spaces on this line. Trim the valance with fringe, cords and tassels or braid.

Awning Valance (Fig. 214): Use two flat extension rods; top rod should have a return of about 2 inches, bottom rod a return of about 8 inches. The rods are placed directly over one another and about 8 inches apart. Cut the fabric to span both rods plus 9 inches in depth for the two casings and scallops. Width should be same as bottom rod plus 3 inches for hems. Turn back ½ inch at each side edge and stitch, then turn back 1-inch hems and sew by hand. Turn back ½ inch at top and bottom edges and stitch. Pin a top hem wide enough to fit over rod, but do not sew. Turn up lower edge with right sides together so that the distance between edges of top and bottom hems will be exactly the same as the distance *between* the rods (Fig. 215). Baste this hem, then mark scallops on the fold, allowing enough fabric above the scallops to form casing (Fig. 216). Stitch on outline of scallops, cut off fabric ½ inch beyond scallops, then clip between scallops and notch curves. Turn to right side and press. Sew on fringe or other trimming. Baste both hems. Try the valance on the rods, *wrong side out*. Pin darts at the corners of the return from top to bottom rods and check the hems to make sure awning will be taut. Remove valance from rods, open hems at darts and stitch darts. Stitch both hems, then stitch below bottom hem to form casing (Fig. 217). Anchor the sides of the awning to window frame with rings and cup hooks placed under the awning.

Cords and Tassels (Fig. 218): These make an attractive finish.

Swags: In spite of their intricate appearance, these are extremely easy to make, even for a beginner. They will add a touch of luxury that cannot be surpassed by any other window treatment and should be combined with very simple curtains or draperies; they can also be used alone over Venetian blinds. Swags also make attractive decorative touches on bedspreads, dressing tables or slipcovers.

Use a solid color, as figured fabric detracts from the lines of the drapery. Suggested fabrics for formal rooms include satin, taffeta, velvet, glossy sateen and brocade; for informal settings try muslin, percale, corduroy or a linen-type fabric. Swags and jabots (or cascades) must be lined. Use a good material because

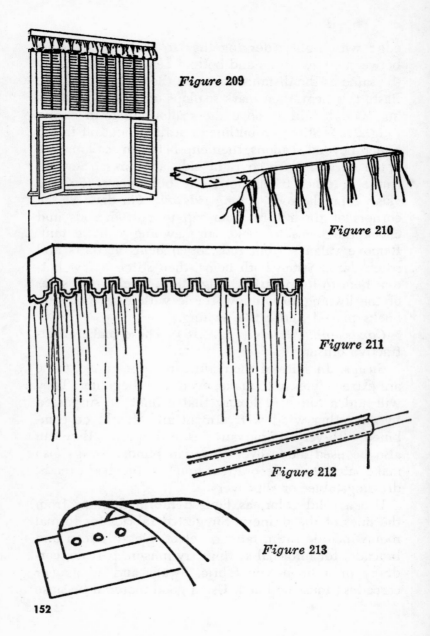

Figure 209

Figure 210

Figure 211

Figure 212

Figure 213

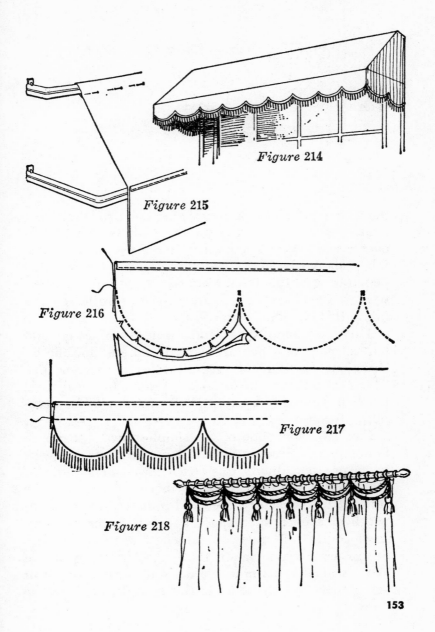

Figure 214

Figure 215

Figure 216

Figure 217

Figure 218

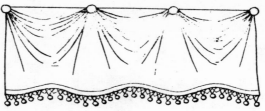

Figure 219

the lining will show. A contrasting color for the lining is most effective, especially on the jabots. When used over a window or lined with a darker color, the main fabric should be heavy enough to keep the light from penetrating or the lining from showing through, otherwise they will need an interlining. Be sure to select a fabric that will drape gracefully.

There are many types and variations of swags and jabots, most of which are described here. Specific instructions for making several styles are given first. These are followed by directions for making swags and jabots in any size for exceptional windows or for decorating furniture.

Fig. 219 shows one of the simplest swags made all in one piece. Measure the width of the space you wish to cover, then divide this space into equal parts for the draped sections. Each of these sections can be from 12 to 24 inches wide. Add 3 inches for the extra width of each draped space and 1 inch for seam allowance; this will give you the length of fabric needed. Swags are always cut on the length of the goods to avoid seams. Determine the desired finished depth of swag, then add 15 inches to this measurement for the

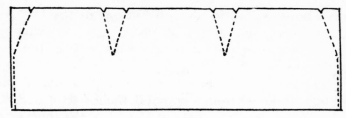

Figure 220

pleats and seam allowance. This will be width of fabric. Cut fabric and lining to these measurements. Place markers across top edge as follows; first marker 2 inches from corner, last marker 2 inches from other corner. Mark off finished width of one draped section, then 3 inches for dart and continue across in this way (Fig. 220). Make a dart on each 3-inch section, taking in the 3 inches on wrong side at top edge and tapering to nothing 14½ inches below top edge. Make darts on lining to correspond. Trim away fabric on darts ½ inch from stitching lines and press seams open. Place fabric and lining with right sides together and darts meeting. Stitch lower edges together, then stitch sides, taking in ½ inch at lower edge and slanting the seams to markers at top as shown on Fig. 220. Trim seam allowance to measure ½ inch, clip off corners of seam allowance and turn swag to right side. Press and sew on any trimming at lower edge. Stitch top edges together. Now place markers on each dart and on each side edge as shown on Fig. 221. Bring top markers to stitching line, then bring second and third markers to meet first markers, forming three sets of pleats. Sew pleats securely in place by hand, overcasting folds on right side and on wrong side (Fig. 222). Sew decorative buttons, fabric-covered buttons or rosettes and tassels over each group of pleats. Mount swag on valance board or on rod in the same way as felt valance on page 150.

Fig. 223 shows a swag with jabots that will fit the average window from about 36 inches to 42 inches wide. The center drop is about 15 inches, the short sides of the jabots are 15 inches and the long edges are 31 inches. Where jabots meet swags, the depth is about 8 inches, so do not mount them too high for the 8-inch corners to cover fixtures, unless these are concealed by curtains. The sides of the swag may be lowered slightly by making the pleats a little farther apart when overlapping them.

For each swag you will need the full width of the material for the depth. Measure the width of the valance board or rod (not counting any return), then add 8 inches for draping. For each pair of jabots you will need the width of the return (side edge of valance board or rod) plus 29 inches. The length required is 64 inches. If the fabric has no right or wrong side, you can save about 12 inches in the length by fitting the diagonal edges together as shown in Fig. 224. If you are making two pairs, you can also save the 12 inches on each pair by cutting them in this way. Remember that there must be a left-hand and a right-hand jabot for each window, and when cut in this way they are identical and cannot be reversed unless the fabric has no right or wrong side. The same amount of lining will be required.

To Make the Swag: Cut fabric and lining to the measurements given in Fig. 225a. Top edge is width of valance board or rod (not including any return);

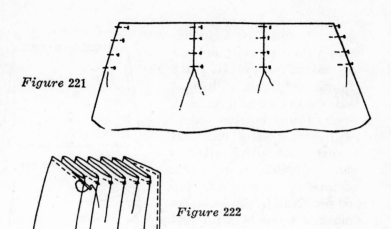

Figure 221

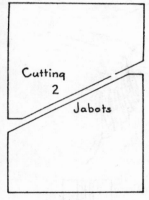

Figure 222

Cutting
2
Jabots

Figure 224

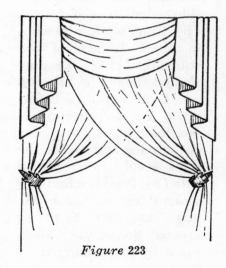

Figure 223

bottom edge is 4 inches wider on each side, so slant the edges out evenly. Place fabric and lining with right sides together and stitch ½ inch from bottom edge. Turn right side out and press. Keeping pieces smooth, stitch on right side ½ inch from side and top edges. Notch the sides to mark the pleats, with first notch about 3 inches from bottom edge and the other notches about 5 inches apart; last notch should be about 5 inches below top stitching line. Fold and pin side edge at each notch (b). Bring top fold to within about ½ inch of top stitching line. Keeping slanted edges even with one another, pin each fold about ½ inch below previous fold. Place swag on a flat surface and crease the folds evenly from side to side (c). Press the folds for about 6 inches at each side edge to hold them as creased. Secure the folds in place by overcasting them

158

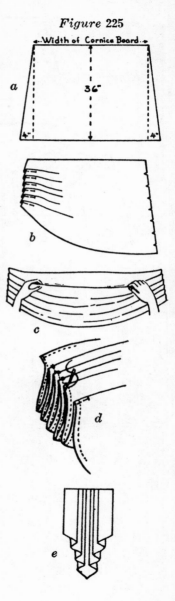

Figure 225

Figure 226

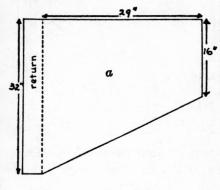

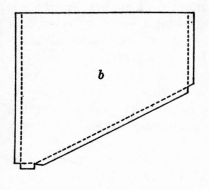

on the stitching line (d), first on right side of swag, then on wrong side; because of the many thicknesses it is impossible to stitch through them on a home sewing machine. Finish the raw edges by binding them with a strip of fabric (e).

To Make the Jabots: Cut fabric and lining to the dimensions given in Fig. 226a. Place fabric and lining with right sides together and stitch ½ inch from side and lower edges, leaving top edge open. Clip off corners of seam allowance (b), turn right side out

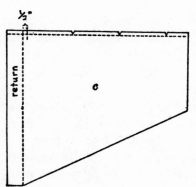

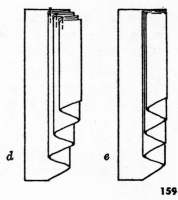

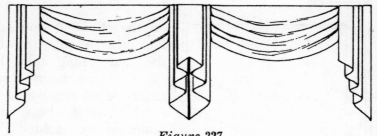

Figure 227

and press. Stitch across top, ½ inch from edge. Mark top of jabot with notches: make the first notch ½ inch beyond the allowance for the return on long edge, then make three more notches 8 inches apart (c). Pin the folds by bringing second notch to meet first notch, then bring each remaining notch to within ½ inch of previous fold (d). If you prefer, the folds can be placed directly over one another with no space between (e). Press the folds thoroughly from top to bottom, then overcast the edges of the folds along the top stitching line in the same way as ends of swag, to hold them firmly in place.

Sew any fringe, braid or trimming to bottom edge of swag and along short side and diagonal edge of jabots.

To Mount Swag and Jabots: If they are to be placed on a rod, sew the three pieces together at the top; jabots will extend beyond the swag on each side to fit over the returns. Turn top edge to wrong side and sew on a casing, keeping swag taut. Casing may be made of fabric or of rug binding (see felt valance on page 150). If they are to be attached to a valance board, sew a piece of tape across the top edges.

Swags and Jabots in Fig. 227: These can be made to cover a group of windows. Make the required number

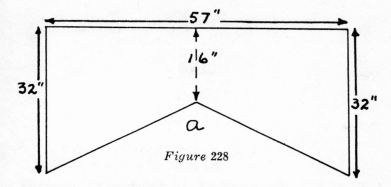

57"

1|6"

32"

32"

a

Figure 228

of swags, one for each window, and a pair of jabots for the two ends.

To Make Double Jabots: Cut fabric and lining to the measurements given in Fig. 228. Place lining and fabric with right sides together and stitch ½ inch from side and lower edges. Clip off seam allowance at corners and snip seam allowance at center between diagonal edges. Turn right side out and press. Pleat each side as shown in Fig. 227 to correspond with the other jabots, omitting the return. Another version is shown in Fig. 229a and b.

Swags and Jabots in Fig. 230: Cut the number of swags desired and cut lining to correspond. With right sides together, join sides of swags, forming one continuous piece (Fig. 231a). Sew lining together in the same way. Press seams. With right sides together, stitch bottom edge, taking in ½-inch seam. Turn to right side and press. Stitch top and side edges together from right side. Notch the edges as for the swag in Fig. 225b, then mark each seam to correspond with notches. Fold sides and seams; folds may overlap one another entirely (Fig. 231b). Seams may be covered

161

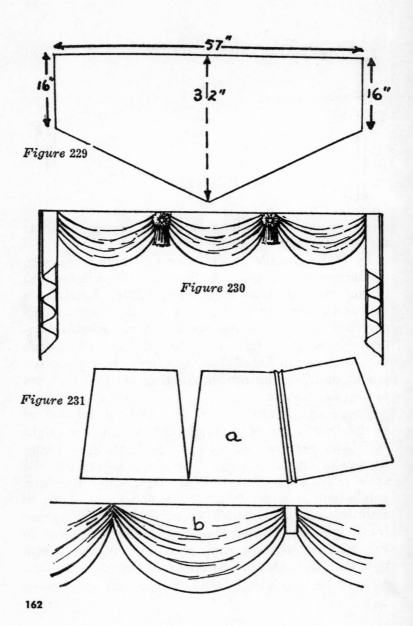

Figure 229

Figure 230

Figure 231

a

b

with rosettes and tassels or with straps of braid or self-fabric. Make the jabots same as for Fig. 226.

Overlapping Swags (Fig. 232): Cut and sew swag and lining same as for Fig. 225. Make notches and pin a fold at each notch. Make pleats at notches, then bring the pleats over the top. Trim edges of pleats even with top of swag.

Festoons on Pole (Fig. 233): Make the two jabots first. Drape a string from A to A on rod (Fig. 234a) to get the measurement for top of swag. Drape another string from B to B for bottom measurement. Cut a length of fabric as long as bottom measurement, then slant both ends so that top will measure same as A to A. Cut lining to correspond. Place fabric and lining with right sides together. Stitch ½ inch from top and bottom edges, turn right side out and press, then stitch side edges together. Pleat ends of swag (see Fig. 225) so that ends of swag will measure same as tops of jabots. Drape sections over rod and pin them together. Remove from rod and sew joinings. To hold them securely on rod, take down rod and make two casings to fit tightly under joinings (Fig. 234b). Fasten festoon to casings by tacking them or with snap tape.

To Make Swags and Jabots Any Size: Try out size by making a pattern of muslin or paper. For small decorative swags, use tissue paper, which is easy to drape. Decide on the depth of the swag when it is draped. This depth will determine all other measurements, so drape the paper or muslin across to see the effect, then measure the following: top edge, bottom edge and center depth. Fig. 235 shows how to make a pattern for cutting the fabric. A to A is the top width, or the space the swag is to cover from side to side.

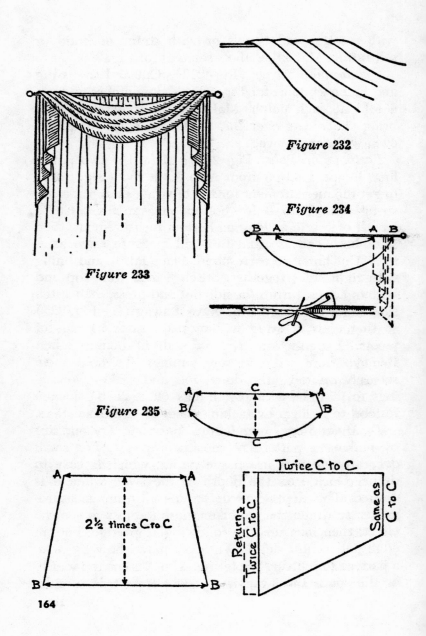

Figure 232

Figure 234

Figure 233

B A   A B

Figure 235

A   C   A

B   B

C

A   A

2½ times C to C

B   B

Twice C to C

Return = Twice C to C

Same as C to C

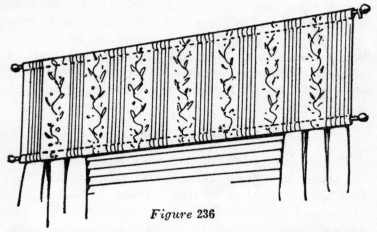

Figure 236

B to B is the bottom curved edge. C to C will be two and one-half times the finished depth of swag. Pleat the sides of the pattern into five or six even folds, then notch the sides at each fold. Cut fabric and lining from this pattern, then complete swag as in Fig. 225.

Make a pattern for the jabots. Short edge will be the same length as finished depth of swag at center; long edge and top edge will be twice this same measurement. Add any return to the width at top (dotted lines on diagram). For a center, or double, jabot, top edge will be four times the center depth of swag, omitting any return. Fold the top edge of pattern into three even pleats and notch each fold. Cut fabric and lining from pattern and complete as for Figs. 226 and 228, or 229.

Valance on Two Rods (Fig. 236): Allowing 3 inches for side hems and 3 inches for top and bottom casings, cut fabric desired width and depth. Turn ½ inch to wrong side on all edges and stitch. Make 1-inch hems on each side, sewing them by hand. Make top and bottom hems to fit over rods, leaving both ends of hems open. Mount valance on top rod, then insert other rod through bottom hem, allowing it to hang free.

LAMBREQUINS

This is the traditional name we have used to differentiate them from cornices and valances, although they are often called by those names.

Made of stiffened fabric, these are shaped like cornices and can be attached to rods or to valance boards. To give them the appearance of cornices, they must extend out from the wall; if they are mounted on rods, the rods will need a return of from 4 to 6 inches.

Like valances, lambrequins are intended to hide all the fixtures and should be deep enough to do so, but not so deep that they will make the window appear top-heavy. Make a paper pattern to determine the best depth.

The fabric can match the draperies or be made of another color that is co-ordinated with the curtaining material or repeats other decorations in the room. The best stiffening is buckram that has been treated to make it impervious to dampness or dry cleaning, such as Permette. Lambrequins can be lined if desired; they may also be padded to give them an upholstered look.

Unlined Lambrequin: Fig. 237 shows a simple lambrequin with a gracefully curved edge. Make a

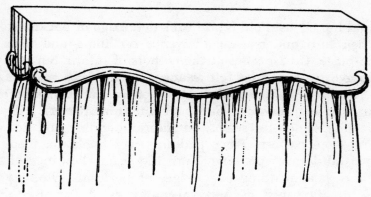

Figure 237

paper pattern, then fold the pattern in half before drawing the outline of the curves, so that when the edge is cut, both sides will be exactly the same. Check the pattern against the window to see the effect. Cut the buckram and fabric from the pattern, allowing ½ inch all around for seams. Pin the buckram to the wrong side of fabric and stitch the edges together, then trim the seam allowance close to the stitching line. Trim the raw edges by covering them with braid, fringe or binding. Crease the corners of the return. Attach to rod or valance board as for the felt valance on page 150.

Lined Lambrequin: Make the paper pattern as for the unlined lambrequin, then cut buckram, fabric and lining from the pattern, allowing ½ inch all around for seams. Pin lining and fabric with right sides together, then place buckram over lining and pin the three thicknesses, keeping them smooth. Stitch lower edge. Trim seam allowance of buckram close to stitching line, then turn right side out with buckram between fabric and lining. Cut off seam allowance of buckram at side

167

and top edges. Fold fabric back over edge of buckram, then turn under seam allowance on lining and sew in place. Crease sides at the corners of return. Sew on tape or casing as for felt valance on page 150.

Padded Lambrequin: Make paper pattern as for unlined lambrequin. Cut buckram from pattern. Allowing ½ inch for seams, cut fabric, padding and lining from pattern. Place padding over buckram, then pin fabric over padding. Turn the seam allowance of fabric and padding over edges of buckram, clipping seam allowance as necessary to keep it flat. Baste securely. Turn back seam allowance on lining and pin lining in place on wrong side. Slip-stitch edges of lining to edges of fabric. Crease sides at corners of return and sew on tape or casing as for felt valance on page 150.

WINDOW SHADES

There is a wide selection of blinds, shades and shutters available on the market, to control light and insure privacy. Some of these are attractive enough so that they can be combined with a simple cornice, valance or festoon to make a handsome window treatment without adding curtains or draperies. There are also at least three kinds that you can make yourself.

Fig. 238 shows a decorative window shade topped by a cornice; Fig. 239 illustrates a Venetian blind under swag and jabots; Fig. 240 tops an Austrian shade with a brass cornice; Fig. 241 shows a Roman shade under lambrequin.

Decorative Window Shade: Old roller shades can be easily replaced with printed fabric, such as glazed

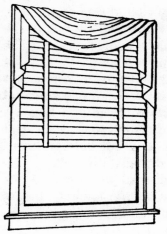

Figure 239

Figure 238

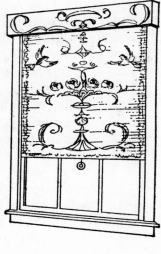

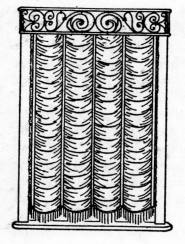

Figure 240

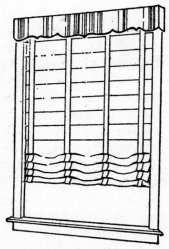

Figure 241

169

chintz. Remove the roller and take off the old shade, marking the position in which it was attached. The fixtures that hold the roller can be reversed by putting the one from the right-hand side on the left; if this is done, the roller will be facing the window and the shade will conceal it. The roller can also be placed at the bottom of the window. A long pull-cord is fastened to the shade and run through an eye screw at the top of the window frame and through another eye screw at the corner. A cleat at the side of the window will hold the cord when the shade is drawn (Fig. 242).

Unfasten the pull-cord and remove the slat from the bottom hem. Allowing 3 inches for making side hems and for a hem at lower edge deep enough to hold the slat, cut *Figure 242* fabric by using the old shade as a pattern. Cut off selvages, then hem the sides so that new shade will fit width of roller exactly; if more than one width is needed, cut one width for the center, then add strips on each side, matching patterns. When stitching the seams or hems, adjust the tension and the length of the stitch so that fabric does not pucker.

Hem lower edge to hold slat. Insert slat and pierce hem for replacing pull-cord. A new cord and an attractive tassel will add to the appearance of your new shade. Tack the shade to the roller, making sure that it faces in the right direction. Use staples or small carpet tacks close together. Wind shade tightly on roller and replace roller.

Another version can have a scalloped hem below the

Figure 243

slat, trimmed with braid or fringe. To make this allow
an extra 12 inches at lower edge. Hem the sides to
fit roller, then turn up the 12-inch allowance at lower
edge to right side. Draw scallops, spacing them evenly
along the fold and leaving enough space above scallops for the hem to hold the slat. Stitch on outline of
scallops, trim seam allowance to measure ½ inch. Clip
seam allowance between scallops and notch curves.
Turn hem right side out, press, then make the casing
for the slat (see Figs. 216 and 217). Sew on fringe.

Roman Shade (Fig. 241): Made of fabric, this is
a window shade that forms even pleats when it is
raised. It requires rings evenly spaced on the wrong
side in rows to guide the cords by which it is raised
and lowered. It can be mounted on a narrow board
secured under the top of the window frame.

Allowing for 2-inch hems, cut fabric to fit inside
measurement of window in width, and about 3 inches
longer than length from board to window sill. Cut off
selvages and hem the sides. Make a hem at lower
edge to hold a rod or slat, which will keep the bottom edge firm and weight the shade. There is a ready-
made tape with rings attached 5 inches apart that
is especially intended for making Roman shades (Fig.
243). Stitch this tape on wrong side of shade, close to
one edge. Keeping rings directly in line with one

another, stitch tape on other edge, then stitch additional rows between, spacing them about 10 to 14 inches apart. On the right side, stitching lines may be hidden by decorative braid or left uncovered.

If you are not using this special tape, stitch horizontal tucks across the fabric, about every 2½ inches as follows. Fold shade with right sides together, 2½ inches above lower edge (Fig. 244), and stitch close to fold. Fold with wrong sides together, 2½ inches above last fold, and stitch

Figure 244

close to fold. Continue to stitch alternately on wrong and right side in this way to the top. Sew a ring to each stitched tuck on the wrong side ½ inch from each edge, then space rings evenly between, about 10 inches apart.

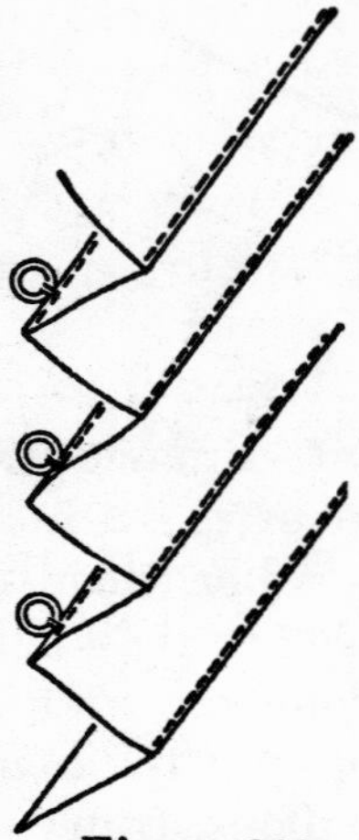

Hem top edge. Mount shade on board, then attach an eye screw (or pulley) directly above each row of rings, and another eye screw, large enough to hold all the cords, at top corner of window. Fasten a cord to the first ring at bottom of shade and thread it through one row of rings to top of shade, then through the eye screw. Thread cords in this way through all rows of rings. Draw all the cords through the eye screw at corner, with each one the proper length to raise shade evenly. Knot them together at top corner with shade lowered, then attach a single cord with a decorative tassel that will be long enough to be reached easily. Attach a cleat to the side of the window (Fig.

242) to hold cord when shade is raised. Insert rod or slat in bottom hem and sew ends of hem.

Austrian Shades (Fig. 240): These are made of soft, sheer fabric and need plenty of fullness to drape gracefully. They can be mounted in the same way as Roman shades. Length of fabric should be three times the length of finished shade; for the width, measure width of window, then add 3 inches for each set of scallops and another 3 inches for the two side hems. (The greater the allowance for the scallops, the deeper they will be.) Each scallop should be about 8 to 10 inches wide when finished, and they must all be the same width; so plan the finished width to fit the window, then add 3 inches allowance for each set of scallops.

If more than one width of fabric is needed, join the widths so that seams will come between scallops; remember to allow 1½ inches on each side for hems. Cut off selvages and join the widths with plain seams. There is a shirring tape (Fig. 245) made especially for Austrian shades, with rings attached to raise and lower the shade. Hem the sides and lower edge. Sew the tape over each side hem on wrong side, starting with a ring at lower edge. Taking care to keep rings directly in line with one another, sew tape between scallops. Stitch fringe across lower edge. Knot the

Figure 245

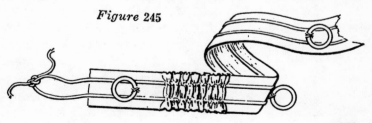

shirring cords at lower edge so they will not pull out, then draw up these cords evenly, gathering shade to desired length and keeping rings directly in line as before. Knot and fasten cords at top. Make darts next to tapes at top, taking in top edge to fit the board. Cover a thin rod with fabric (see Fig. 234b) to fit across the bottom of shade. Slide rod through the bottom row of rings and tack to shade at ends. Fasten a cord to each bottom ring and thread it through the rings to the top. Mount shade and fasten cords in the same way as for Roman shades.

Bedspreads

TYPES OF BEDS

There are five basic kinds of beds, each of which must be treated differently:

Studio Couch: This needs a cover that will reach to the floor on all four sides. If it is used in a bedroom, the spread can be made long enough to tuck under the pillows; if it is used as a seating unit in a living room the pillows are removed in the daytime and the cover is made to fit over the mattress. Matching bolsters or cushions will give it the appearance of a sofa (Fig. 246).

Hollywood Bed: Originally this name referred to twin beds with one headboard; the beds were hinged to swing out for ease in bed-making. Now, the term has come to mean any bed without footboard or side rails. This type of bed needs a spread that will cover three sides with the skirt, or flounce, in one continuous piece (Fig. 247).

Beds with Posts or Open Footboards: The bedspread must cover the foot of the bed and be shaped to fit around the posts (Figs. 248 and 249).

Daybeds and Beds with Closed Footboards: Daybeds have headboard and footboard of the same height and can be used against a wall to serve as a sofa. In

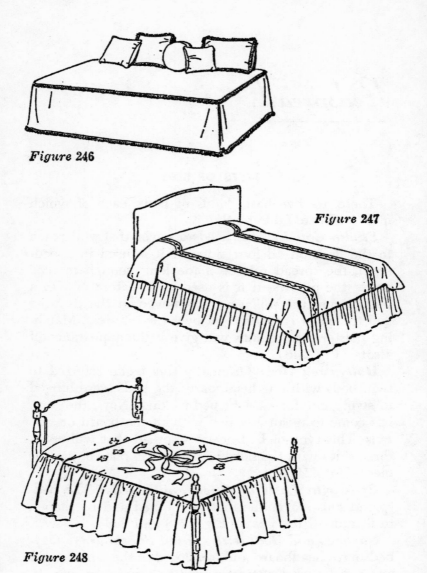

Figure 246

Figure 247

Figure 248

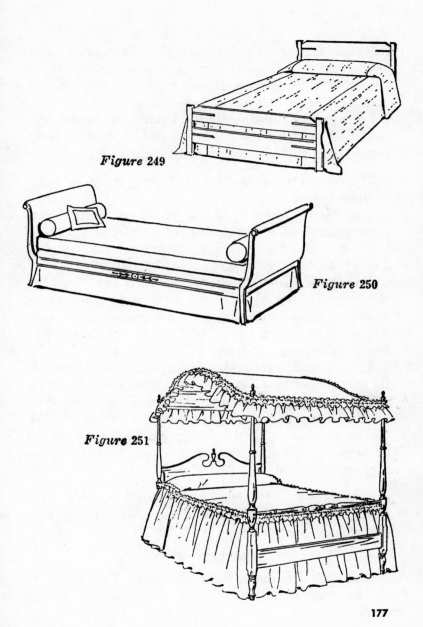

Figure 249

Figure 250

Figure 251

177

this case, they can be slip-covered in the same way as a sofa and the mattress is treated as a cushion (Fig. 250). When there is a closed footboard, the spread need only cover the top and the sides.

Four-Poster Canopy Beds: These are usually covered with a sheer ruffled bedspread or a fitted bedspread with ruffled flounces (Fig. 251).

There are also several kinds of bedspreads for each of these types:

One-Piece Throw Spreads: These are unfitted and large enough to cover the top and sides of the bed. They can also be shaped to fit around posts at the foot of the bed (Figs. 252 and 253).

One-Piece Fitted Spreads: There is one piece for the top of the bed, outlined with welting or other trimming around the edge of the mattress. A skirt, flounce or ruffle is attached to the top section and falls to the floor (Figs. 254 and 255).

Two-Piece Spreads: A separate skirt, flounce or ruffle is attached to a piece of muslin or a sheet, which is placed under the mattress to conceal the box spring when the top part of the bedspread is removed. The top of the bed is then covered with a throw spread or fitted spread that need only cover the top of the flounce (Fig. 256).

Other kinds of bedspreads are studio-couch covers, formal treatment for daybeds and sheer ruffled bedspreads and canopie

MATTRESS SIZES

Mattress sizes have been changing. The height of the average American is increasing, and tall people need long beds. The three-quarter bed, which used to be popular, is becoming rare. Here is a list of the various sizes:

Twin Size	39 x 75	inches
Three-Quarter Size	48 x 75	inches
Double Size	54 x 75	inches
Twin Long Boy	39 x 80	inches
Double Long Boy	54 x 80	inches
Queen Size	60 x 80	inches
King Size	75 x 80	inches
Giant Size	78 x 80	inches

ONE-PIECE THROW SPREAD

The fabric for this should be firm enough to hold its shape and is used on the length of the goods for all sections.

Yardage: Measure the length of the mattress. If the bedspread is to cover the foot of the bed, add the length from top of mattress to the floor (Fig. 257). Add 27 inches to cover the pillow—for extra thickness of double pillows, add 36 inches. Add 2 inches for hems. You will need one length for the center of the bedspread, plus one or one and one-half lengths on each side to reach to the floor, depending on the width of the bed and the width of the fabric. Allow 2 inches for seams; selvage must be removed before joining lengths. If using a patterned fabric, add one repeat of the design for each additional length. Enough lining will be needed to line entire spread.

Trimming: The seams between the lengths can be

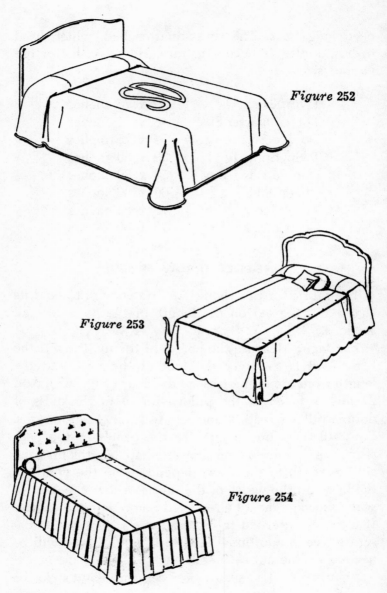

Figure 252

Figure 253

Figure 254

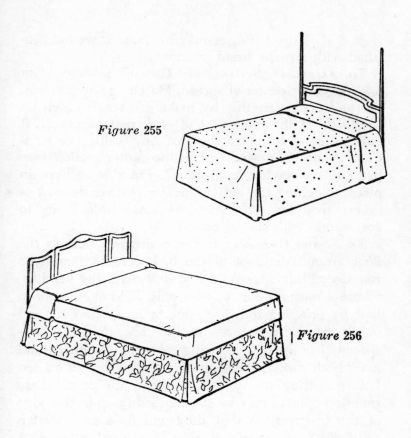

Figure 255

| *Figure 256*

Figure 257

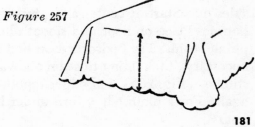

welted if desired. Edges may be bound, welted, finished with a ruffle, braid or fringe.

To Assemble Bedspread: Cut off selvages. Cut one length for center of spread. Matching any patterns, cut additional lengths; by making a small notch on each side at the same part of each pattern repeat, it will be easier to match designs. Any welting or trimming should be sewed first to the center section (see page 47 for sewing on welting). Pin side sections in place, matching the patterns and any up-and-down of fabric, then sew (see page 53). Assemble lining to correspond with size of spread.

To Shape Corners: If the bedspread falls to the floor around the foot of the bed, corners should be rounded. Place spread on bed and mark the hemline, where it meets the floor, with pins. Fold one corner in half by bringing the side edge to meet the end, and check the curve to even it smoothly. Fold the bedspread lengthwise, bringing corners together, and mark both corners the same. Try the bedspread on bed before cutting off excess. If there are posts, these rounded corners may be slit diagonally up to the edge of the mattress, so that they will flare and overlap (Fig. 258), or the corners may be cut out, allowing 1 inch for hems (Fig. 259).

To Line Bedspread: Pin lining to bedspread, right sides out. Start at center and pin securely from top to bottom. Place on floor and smooth lining to the seams, pin at seams. Try bedspread on bed and adjust pins if necessary. Tack lining to seam allowance with skeleton stitches (Fig. 260). Pin edges together and try on bed again. For a plain edge, turn under hem allowance on

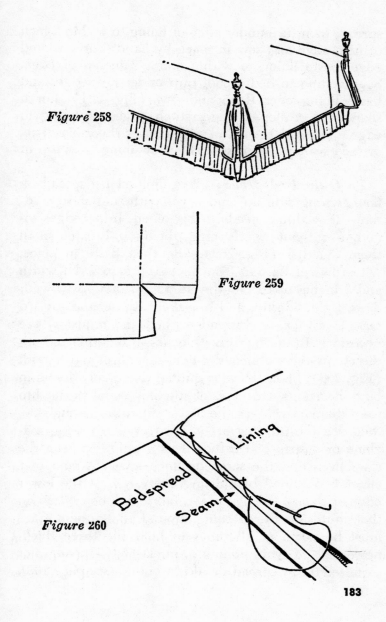

Figure 258

Figure 259

Lining

Bedspread

Seam

Figure 260

183

spread, then turn under edge of lining to within ½ inch of hem edge and sew in place by hand. For a welted edge, baste lining to within about 2 inches of edge. Sew welting to bedspread, turn under raw edges and baste lining over them and sew (Fig. 261). For a shaped or scalloped edge, stitch edges of lining to edges of spread, then bind with a bias strip or bias tape, or face scallops, then sew edges of lining over top of facing.

To Quilt Bedspread: Place unlined bedspread on floor, wrong side up, and cover with thin sheet-wadding. If wadding needs to be joined, bring edges together without overlapping them, and catch-stitch them together (Fig. 262). Pin, then baste in place, with rows of basting 3 inches apart across the width and 3 inches apart lengthwise. Place lining over wadding, right side up, and pin along center and toward both sides. Try bedspread on bed and adjust where necessary. Baste the three thicknesses together in both directions every 3 inches to hold them firm and smooth (Fig. 263). Plain fabric is quilted diagonally across in both directions with rows of stitching evenly spaced to form diamonds. Mark the first row on the wrong side, then use the quilting attachment on the sewing machine or a strip of cardboard as a guide to keep the rows even and the same distance apart. A smoother effect is obtained by starting every row at the lower edge of the spread. Patterned fabric can be quilted on the right side by stitching around the design. Care must be taken at all times to hold the three thicknesses flat, to avoid pulling or puckering. The edges of a quilted throw spread should be bound (see page 199).

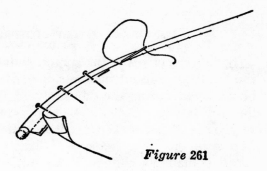

Figure 261

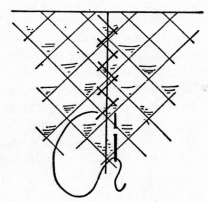

Figure 262

Figure 263

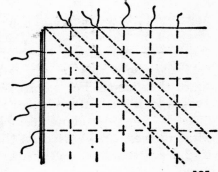

ONE-PIECE FITTED BEDSPREAD

To fit perfectly, the bedspread should be made over the mattress without blankets. The blankets must then be removed during the daytime and replaced at night. Since different weights of bedding are used in various seasons and are tucked in differently each day, it is impossible to fit a bedspread exactly over bedding. Electric blankets cannot be properly covered with a fitted bedspread. However, allowance can be made by fitting the spread over the average amount of bedding, although it will never fit perfectly. In other words, you have the choice between a handsome fitted bedspread during the day, or the convenience of leaving blankets on the bed under a less well-fitting coverlet.

Yardage: Measure the length of the mattress. To this, add 27 inches for covering pillows—for extra thickness of double pillows, add 36 inches—plus 2 inches for hem and seam. You will need one length for center top of spread, and one length split in half or two lengths for the sides. For a patterned fabric, add the length of one repeat of design for each additional length. For the skirt, measure the depth from top of mattress to floor, then add 3 inches for hem and seam; this will be width of skirt. Measure around the bed for the length. A ruffled skirt should be two and one-half to three times this length, a box-pleated skirt three times this length. For a skirt with kick pleats you will need a kick pleat at each corner and one at the center of each long side; allow 16 inches for each kick pleat. Most fabrics can be used on the lengthwise grain, but if the pattern has a very distinct up-and-down that would be unattractive with the figures turned sideways, you will need about 8 widths for a kick-pleated skirt. All sections must have patterns matched exactly, so allow for this. A ruffled or box-pleated skirt will require enough widths to fit three times around the sides and foot of the bed; however, designs need not match at seams. If the top of the bedspread is made of heavy or quilted material, it is best to use a matching or co-ordinated fabric of lighter weight for a ruffled or pleated skirt; if the skirt is also to be made of the heavy fabric, make simulated kick pleats (Fig. 264)—see instructions on page 59—and bind the edges. You will need enough lining to measure same as bedspread.

Trimming: The top section should be outlined with welting (Fig. 265), reverse French seams (see page 26) or other trimming. A ruffled skirt can be finished with a heading to form this outline (Fig. 266). If so, allow 2 inches for a top hem on the skirt.

To Assemble Bedspread: Cut off all selvages. Cut a length for the center of the top section, then cut two strips to complete the desired width of mattress, matching any patterns. Sew the sections together; these seams are usually not welted. Place top of spread on bed, with center section at center of mattress. With chalk or pins, mark the exact edge of bed or bedding, curving the corners to follow lines of mattress—look at the mattress and you will see that it is not squared off at the corners, but gently rounded. Sew welting or other trimming around this line (see page 47 for sewing on welting). If there is a pillow, no trimming will be needed at the head of the spread. Join skirt sections, matching any patterns if necessary for a kick-pleated

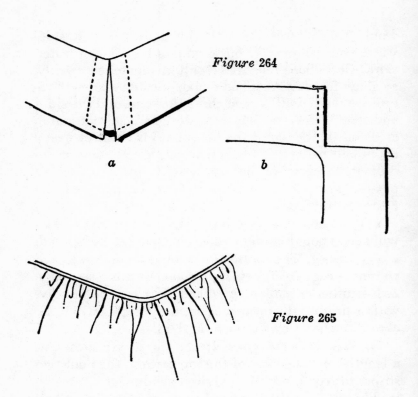

Figure 264

a   *b*

Figure 265

Figure 266

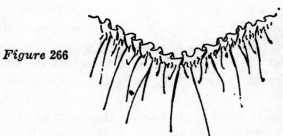

skirt; for simulated kick pleats or for a bed with posts, assemble each section separately.

If you wish to scallop the edge of the skirt, see page 200; otherwise, cut lining 3 inches shorter than skirt. Line skirt by sewing bottom edges together on wrong side. Turn right side out and bring top edges together, forming a 1½-inch hem. Baste top edges together and press. Finish ends of skirt or skirt sections in the same way as for simulated kick pleats (page 59).

To Attach Skirt:

Kick Pleats: Pin center of skirt to center at foot of bedspread, right sides together. Pin to corners, making a 4-inch pleat on each side of both corners. Pin ends of skirt to head of bedspread. Find center of mattress on one long side; this is the point at which the center pleat will be made on skirt. Pin from both ends toward this point, then fold excess to form center kick pleat (Fig. 267). Stitch to top section as pinned.

Box Pleats: Starting at center, make a box pleat on skirt by folding fabric and placing a pin 4 inches from fold at top edge. Skip 6 inches, make another fold and

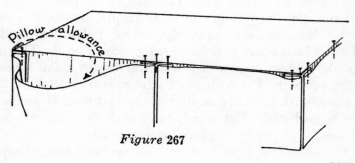

Figure 267

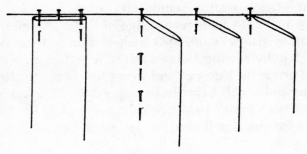

Figure 268

pin 4 inches from fold (Fig. 268). Continue in this way toward both ends. Measure resulting length and, if necessary, place pins farther apart by making folds less deep. Open up each fold and flatten. Pin box pleats in place at top of skirt, then baste or stitch to hold them firm and even. Sew skirt to top section, right sides together.

Ruffled Skirt: If heading is to be used (see Fig. 266), hem top edge of skirt. Line top section of bedspread (see page 182), and finish edges by turning under seam allowance of lining over raw edges of fabric. Sew shirring tape to wrong side of skirt, just covering base of top hem, or make rows of stitching below hem and about ½ inch apart to hold shirring tape or cords. There should be two or more rows of shirring to make ruffle hang properly. Pin corners of skirt to corners at foot of spread, with base of heading at marked line. Draw up cords, gathering skirt evenly to fit each side, and pin in place. Stitch ruffle in place on right side.

If no heading is to be used, sew welting around top

of bedspread. Gather raw edge at top of skirt; if you are using the sewing machine attachment, adjust it so that it will gather the fabric to the desired fullness. To gather skirt by hand, run two rows of heavy duty thread ¼ inch apart and ½ inch from top of skirt for 1 yard. Draw up these threads to measure 18 inches for double fullness, 12 inches for triple fullness. Continue to gather each yard in this way, then stitch gathers in place between the threads, distributing fullness evenly. Sew ruffle to bedspread, right sides together.

Simulated Kick Pleats: Make a separate section for end of bed and two sections for each long side; the simulated pleat on the long side should be planned to come at center of mattress. Finish ends of each section (see page 59), then stitch to top of spread. Make an 8-inch flap to fit under each opening and sew in place.

To Line Top of Bedspread: Turn all raw edges to the center and press. Pin lining to top section, right side out. Try on bed to make sure lining lies smoothly. Turn under seam allowance on lining and sew by hand over raw edges of skirt.

TWO-PIECE BEDSPREADS

The flounce, or skirt, is sewn to a separate piece of muslin or an old sheet that fits under the mattress. The top of the bed is then covered with a throw spread or fitted spread that reaches below the top of the flounce.

To Measure Yardage: Depth of flounce will be 3 inches longer than distance from top of box spring to floor to allow for hem and seam. Measure the yardage to this width in the same way as skirt for one-piece fitted bedspreads. Top section of bedspread can be measured as for one-piece throw or fitted spread, allowing for the shorter length; the average top section will reach to within about 12 inches of floor, depending on the height of bed. You will need the same amount of lining as fabric, plus the muslin or sheet to cover top of box spring. If desired, add enough fabric to make a 4-inch border around the top of the box spring cover.

To Make Box-Spring Cover (Fig. 269): Cut and join two or more lengths of muslin, or cut an old sheet, to make a piece 1 inch larger than top of box spring. *Cut corners square.* Custom-made box spring covers have 4 inches of the edge concealed by strips of the main fabric. To do this, cut 4-inch strips same length as each side of the muslin. Pin these strips, right side up, to outer edges of muslin. Miter corners smoothly. Stitch outer edges together, turn under ½ inch at inner edges and top-stitch in place. Round off the corners to fit curve of box spring (Fig. 270) and stitch. Outer edges can now be welted, if desired, although this is not necessary. Make flounce same as skirt for one-piece fitted spreads and join to box spring cover. Make top section as for one-piece bedspreads, long enough to cover top of flounce (Figs. 271 and 272).

STUDIO-COUCH COVERS

These can be made like throw spreads to reach to the floor around all four sides. Each corner should then be rounded. Or, they can be made like fitted bedspreads, with the skirt continuing around both ends. To give them the appearance of sofas, they should be

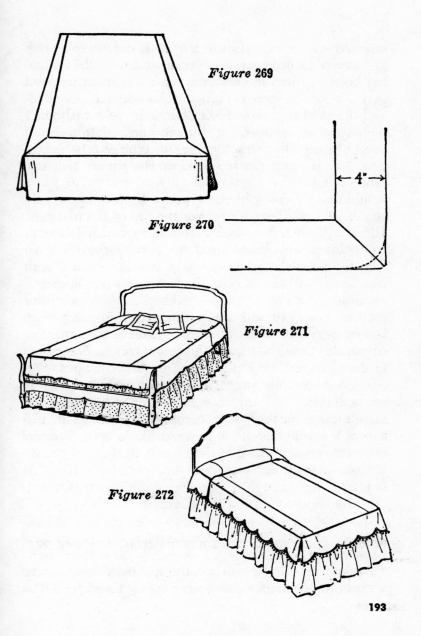

Figure 269

Figure 270

4"

Figure 271

Figure 272

covered with sturdy fabric that will not rumple. Fig. 273 shows a studio couch covered with felt. The matching bolsters provide greater comfort for a seating unit and add to the general effect. The edges are welted, and the skirt is trimmed with bands of velvet ribbon 2 inches wide, mitered at the corners. Cotton braid would be equally attractive for this type of ornamentation. The trimming is repeated on the square bolsters. Since felt can be obtained in 2-yard widths, 6 yards would make a cover of this type for the average studio couch. Use one length to cover the top of the mattress, allowing 1 inch for seams. The extra width left over from this piece can be used for part of the skirt. To trim the panels, mark position of ribbon or braid with chalk and yardstick about 5 inches from seam lines and hemline. Stitch outer edge of ribbon to this line, miter corners, then pin and stitch inner edge in place. Fig. 246 on page 176 shows another version of the same felt cover; this time the trimming is moss fringe. The couch is then heaped with pillows of different shapes. Fig. 274 gives another suggestion for this type of cover: cords and tassels form festoons around the top and the tassels are repeated on the round bolsters. Fig. 275 shows a studio couch slipcovered like a sofa. Bolsters are hung on a rod fastened to the wall. Follow the instructions for fitted one-piece bedspreads; if the skirt is made long enough, a box under the couch can contain the bedding during the daytime.

FORMAL TREATMENT FOR DAYBEDS (Figs. 276 and 277)

Make a cushion cover for the mattress in the same way as for chair cushion (see pages 45 and 61). The

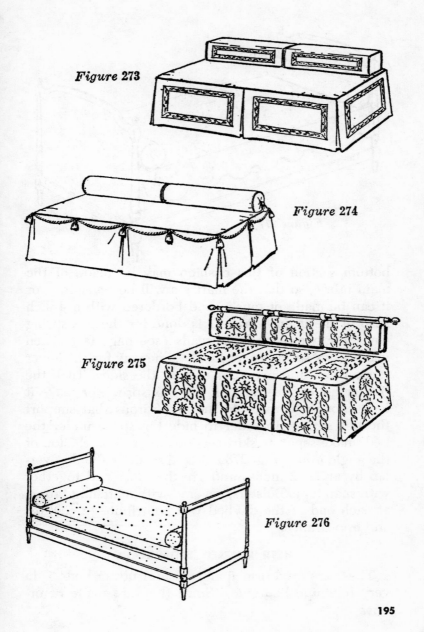

Figure 273

Figure 274

Figure 275

Figure 276

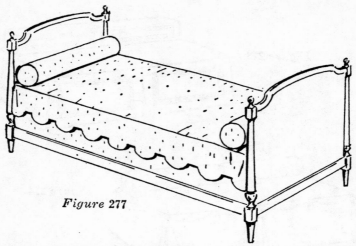

Figure 277

bottom section of this cushion may be made of the main fabric, so that the mattress will be reversible, or it can be made of muslin and bordered with a 4-inch strip of the main fabric, as is done for the box-spring cover for two-piece bedspreads (see page 00). Then make a box-spring cover in the same way for the lower section and add a border around the sides. Tack the border under the frame of the box spring, or make it long enough to reach to the angle irons that support the box spring. In order to hide the space under the bed, make separate skirt sections to fit on each side of the angle irons (Fig. 278). These sections should overlap by about 2 inches and are then fastened together with snap tape. Bolsters, covered with matching fabric, at each end of the daybed will contribute to comfort and appearance.

SHEER RUFFLED BEDSPREADS

These are used principally for four-poster beds or in very feminine bedrooms. Since they are made of or-

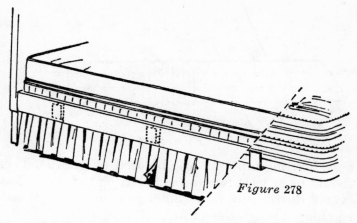

Figure 278

gandy, dotted swiss or other material that needs frequent washing, starching and ironing, they are placed over a separate lining. The lining is usually made of sateen in the form of a plain, unlined throw spread to cover the bedding and pillows, then is hemmed on all four sides. Sheer fabric requires more fullness than other materials and needs ruffled flounces. These ruffles are then frequently trimmed with narrow ruffles, which can be repeated along the edges of the mattress (see Fig. 251 on page 177). Follow directions for fitted bedspreads, making either one-piece or two-piece style. Cut ruffles on the straight of goods to about three or four times the desired finished length. Join strips with narrow French seams (Fig. 162 on page 121), then make ¼-inch hems on both edges. Ruffles can be gathered at center or near one edge to give the effect of a heading on one side. Sheer fabric can be gathered by hand, by using heavy thread and basting stitch on the sewing machine, or with the ruffling attachment that has been adjusted to gather material to the desired full-

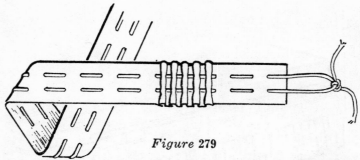

Figure 279

ness. Shirring tape can also be used (Fig. 279). There should be at least two rows of shirring to keep fullness evenly distributed. Sew ruffles in place on right side, stitching through the gathers.

CANOPIES

Two or three lengths of fabric are joined together lengthwise to cover the top of the frame. The top section may be lined; if no lining is used, fabric should be joined with felled seams (Fig. 163 on page 121). Ruffles are sewed to the top section, overlapping around the posts. If properly fitted, the canopy will stay in place. Fasten overlapping edges with snap tape.

TRIMMING FOR BEDSPREADS

Scalloped Edges: Patterns for scallops and other decorative shaped edges are available at pattern counters. You can also make your own pattern for simple scallops by tracing the outline of a bowl, butter plate, saucer, or other round object about 5 or 6 inches across, on a piece of cardboard. Cut out this circle, then cut it in half for pattern. Mark the exact center of curved edge for tip of scallop. Draw a line with chalk on edge of bedspread for bottom of scallops, curving the line smoothly around curved corners. Mark center of bedspread at foot of bed or on one long side. Starting at center point, divide edge into equal spaces approximately the same width as straight edge of scallop pattern. Place tip of pattern on center mark and draw outline with chalk. Move pattern with tip on next mark and draw outline. Continue in this way toward each end; there should be a full scallop at each corner and a half scallop at each end. Fig. 280 shows how scallops may overlap slightly if spaces are smaller than pattern; Fig. 281 shows how scallops can be connected by straight lines if spaces are slightly larger than pattern. The corners are more important than the head of the bedspread, which will be hidden; on a studio couch, the two front corners are the most important.

For Lining a Scalloped Skirt cut lining same depth as skirt. Place lining and fabric with right sides together. Mark the scallop pattern on lining, then stitch along marked line. Trim seam allowance to ½ inch (Fig. 282). Clip into the seam allowance at corners between scallops and notch the curved edges (Fig. 283). Turn to right side and press on stitching line.

Bound Edges: Use bias tape in matching or coordinated color, or a bias strip of self-fabric (see page 48). Place edge of bias at edge of fabric, right sides together and raw edges meeting. Stitch in place, then trim seam allowance to measure about ¼ inch. Turn back bias over this seam allowance and hem in place by hand on wrong side, turning in raw edge. *For binding scalloped edge,* trim seam allowance on scallops to measure ½ inch, then bind edge same as for plain edge, taking care that bias stays flat when turning corners between scallops; if necessary, clip the seam allowance of bias slightly so that it will stretch around corners. Trim seam allowance to ¼ inch, turn back bias over this seam allowance, folding it neatly at corners, turn under raw edge and hem by hand on wrong side (Fig. 284).

Fringe: There are many types of fringe in cotton or rayon and in a wide range of colors and color combinations. Instead of sewing fringe to the edge of bed-

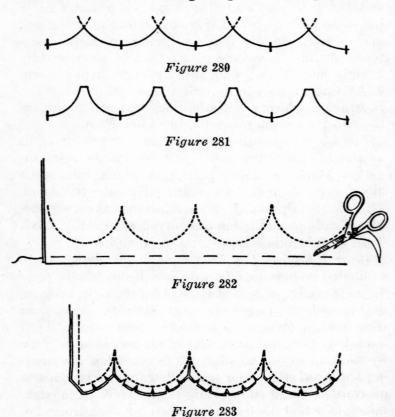

Figure 280

Figure 281

Figure 282

Figure 283

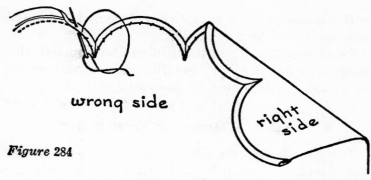

wrong side

right side

Figure 284

spread, try placing it above the edge so that the lower edge of fringe is even with hemline or slightly above it (Fig. 285). Rows of fringe can also be used for a uxurious effect on plain fabric.

Braid: Strips of braid can be used to cover the seams on a throw spread or to make designs on a plain skirt (see Fig. 247 on page 176).

Welting or Cording: Thick, or jumbo, cording makes a wide roll on the edge of the bedspread, similar to the roll at the hem of a Japanese kimono. Although this is not available in stores, you may be able to get it from your local upholsterer. Rows of narrow cording or welting (Fig. 286) can be made in self-fabric, in different shades of one color or in variegated colors to repeat the colors in the pattern or in other parts of the room. Make the welting yourself; commercial welting does not have a wide enough seam allowance for the rows to overlap. Cut bias strips about 2 inches wide (see page 48 for covering cord). Sew the first row of welting far enough from the edge to leave room for the other rows, with raw edges always toward the outer edge of the spread (Fig. 287). The last set of raw edges is turned under on wrong side and covered with the lining, which is sewed in place by hand to the last row of stitching (Fig. 288).

Festoons: The top of the skirt can be trimmed with swags and jabots (Fig. 289). To make these any desired size, see directions on page 163.

TO MAKE A BEDSPREAD WITH SHEETS

Use two sheets 81 x 108 inches. Cut one length for top of bed; this piece should be width of mattress plus 1 inch for seams, and length of mattress plus 27 inches for tucking it under the pillows. Cut remainder of the same sheet into a 25-inch strip. Cut the other sheet into three lengths 25 inches wide. Join the four strips and hem one long edge; finished width should be about the same as height of bed. Gather top edge to fit around top section at sides and foot of bed, distributing fullness evenly, or sew shirring tape on wrong side. Sew ruffle to top section with right sides together, taking in ½-inch seam. Hem top edge.

COVERS FOR BED PILLOWS

There are several ways of concealing the bed pillows besides folding the bedspread over them. They can be placed inside a wooden bolster, which has been covered with fabric to match the spread (Fig. 290), under a separate coverlet (Fig. 291), or under a flap attached to the head of the bedspread and folded back over them (Fig. 292), or they can be inserted in pillow shams (Fig. 293).

Wooden Bolsters: To cover one of these, stretch a piece of fabric over the center section, tacking the

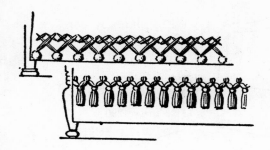

Figure 285

Figure 286

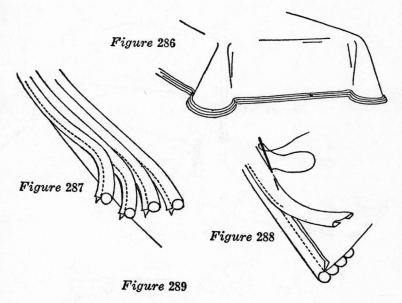

Figure 287

Figure 288

Figure 289

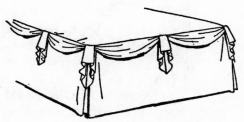

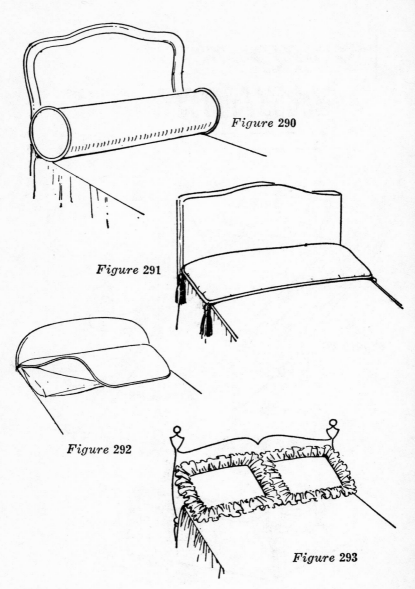

Figure 290

Figure 291

Figure 292

Figure 293

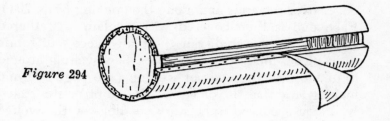

Figure 294

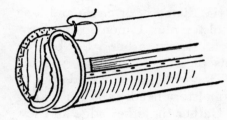

Figure 295

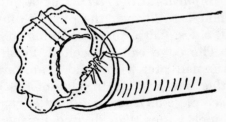

Figure 296

Figure 297

edges over the ends and along the opening (Fig. 294). Each end is then covered with a plain or gathered circle of the material. For the plain piece, cut fabric to fit plus ½-inch seam allowance. Sew welting around the edge, splicing ends of welting (see page 50) and making sure that the piece will fit end of bolster exactly. Using a curved upholstery needle, sew the welted edge in place, hiding the stitches under the welting (Fig. 295). For the gathered piece, cut a strip of fabric 1 inch wider than half the diameter of circle and long enough to fit around bolster plus 1 inch seam allowance. Join the ends to fit exactly around the bolster. Finish one edge of this piece with welting, splicing the ends of welting (see page 50). Sew welted edge to bolster, using curved upholstery needle and concealing stitches under welting. Gather the other edge and sew tightly together. Cover the center with a rosette and tassel (Figs. 296 and 297).

Separate Coverlet: Cut a piece of fabric large enough to fit over the pillows plus about 4 inches on all sides. Cut a piece of lining to correspond.

The edge can be welted, finished with a ruffle, or trimmed later with braid, gimp or fringe. *For a welted edge,* sew welting to edge of fabric, splicing the ends (see page 50). *For a ruffled edge,* cut a strip of fabric 1 inch wider than desired finished width and two or three times the circumference of coverlet. Join the ends, then make a narrow hem along one edge. Gather other edge to fit around coverlet, then baste in place with right sides together and raw edges meeting (Fig. 298). Stitch ½ inch from edge.

Now place lining and fabric with right sides together and baste. Leaving an opening about 10 inches long on

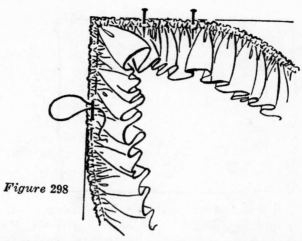

Figure 298

one side, stitch together; if there is welting or a ruffle, stitch directly over previous stitching line. Turn coverlet right side out and sew opening. A plain edge can now be trimmed with gimp, braid or fringe. If they are appropriate for the type of decor, add tassels to each corner.

Flaps: Make these in the same way as the coverlets, trimming edges with welting or braid. Then sew one long edge to center top of bedspread with right side of flap on wrong side of spread, so that the right side of flap will be uppermost when it is turned back over the pillows.

Pillow Shams: These are decorative pillow cases made to match the bedspread and are usually finished with a flange (Fig. 299) or with a ruffle. The back has an opening that can be closed with a zipper slightly shorter than one end of the pillow, with snap fasteners or with buttons and buttonholes.

For a flange cut the top section about 9 inches longer

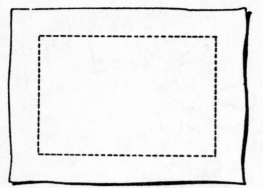

Figure 299

and 9 inches wider than pillow; this will allow for a 3-inch flange and 1-inch leeway all around so that the sham will not fit pillow too tightly. *If the opening is to be closed with a zipper,* cut the back section 1½ inches longer than top section, then cut this piece straight across about 5½ inches from one short edge (Fig. 300). Baste these cut edges together again, taking in ¾-inch seam. Measure off the length of the zipper at the center of this seam and mark. Stitch the ends of the seam beyond the marks, leaving center basted for inserting zipper. Press seam open. Place seam right side up over

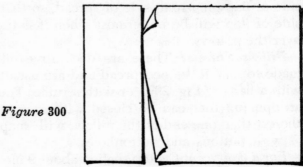

Figure 300

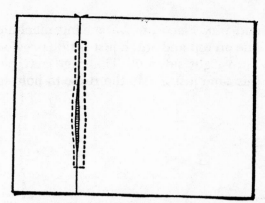

Figure 301

right side of zipper with one edge close to zipper teeth. Stitch along this edge, across end of zipper (Fig. 301), then ½ inch from seam along other side and across other end. Remove bastings and open zipper. *If buttons or snap fasteners are to be used,* cut back section 5 inches longer than top section. Cut this piece across, about 6 inches from one short end, then make 2-inch hems on each side of these cut edges. Overlap the hems so that both sections of sham will be the same size. Place the sections right sides together and pin. Stitch ½ inch from edge all around. Turn sham right side out, then stitch 3 inches from edge. Make buttonholes and sew on buttons, or sew on snap fasteners.

For a ruffled edge cut top section 1½ inches longer and 1½ inches wider than pillow; this allows ½-inch seam allowance and 1-inch leeway all around so that sham will not fit pillow too tightly. Cut back section in same way as for flange, depending on whether zipper or other type of closing will be used, then sew in zipper or hem edges of opening in same way. Make ruffle and attach to top of sham as for coverlet on page 206. Place top and back sections with right sides together

209

and pin. Place on the sewing machine with stitching line on top and stitch just inside previous stitching line. Turn right side out. The edge may be stitched again, this time just inside the ruffle to hold it flat.

Dressing Tables

THE CHARMING femininity of a dressing table can be the crowning touch to a bedroom or a guest room (Fig. 302). When a young girl achieves a dressing table of her own, she feels truly glamorous and grown up. A dressing table, be it ever so tiny, in the powder room will bid your guests welcome.

You can buy a dressing table, transform an old one or make one out of a table, sewing machine or a small desk. You can even assemble a few simple materials to make an admirable substitute.

Two small composition chests, like those used for storing shoes, with a board nailed across them (Fig. 303), can be masked with a taffeta skirt, covered with a mirror top cut to fit—these are surprisingly inexpensive—and provided with a framed mirror.

If you have a space between two windows, the mirrored board can be fastened to the window sills and the entire wall space between the windows covered with another mirror, as shown in Fig. 304.

Another suggestion is the corner dressing table; in this case, a triangular or wedge-shaped board is fastened to the wall with angle irons (Fig. 305), and two mirrors complete the effect of a dressing table.

Figure 302

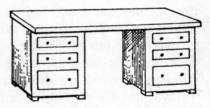

Figure 303

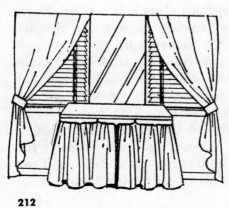

Figure 304

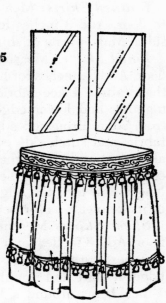

Figure 305

Select a fabric for the skirt like the bedspread, the curtains or slipcovers, or one that will co-ordinate with the colors in the room. Avoid headings around the top as they collect powder and hairpins and are difficult to keep immaculate. A dressing table needs knee room. If there is drawer space underneath, make the skirt in two sections for easy access to the drawers; otherwise, it can be made in one piece and can conceal a wastepaper basket or storage boxes.

Sheer fabric will need triple fullness, double hems and a separate lining. Other fabrics can have double or triple fullness, depending on their weight, and can be lined or unlined. The skirt can reach around the entire table or around only the part that shows. Most dressing table skirts are shirred, although they may be pleated, box pleated or made with flounces. They should be mounted on a band of matching or contrasting fabric that has been stiffened with canvas, pellon or buckram so that it will hold its shape. The band can be straight or shaped. The band on sheer material will need an interlining of the same fabric as skirt lining to keep the stiffening from showing through.

213

Unlined Skirts: Measure the length from table top to floor. Add 3 inches for hem. Hem lower edge and sides. Make pleats or shirring as for bedspread skirt.

Lined Skirts: Measure length from top of table to floor. Add 3½ inches for hem; cut lining 6 inches shorter than fabric. Place fabric and lining with right sides together and lower edges meeting and stitch ½ inch from edge. Bring top edges together, forming hem on fabric, and stitch side edges. Clip off corners of seam allowance and turn right side out. Press, then baste top edges. Measure from hem to top for desired finished length and trim top edge if necessary. Shirr top edge or make pleats as for bedspread skirts.

Sheer Skirts: Measure length from top of table to floor. Add 8 inches for a double 4-inch hem. Cut lining 7 inches shorter than fabric. Make double hem at lower edge of skirt and double 2-inch hems at sides. Make 1-inch hems around side and lower edges of lining; lining should be ½ inch shorter than skirt. Skirt and lining may be shirred separately or basted together and shirred.

Figure 306 *a*

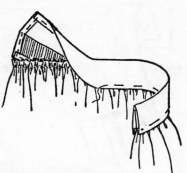

Figure **306 b**

Straight Band: Cut a strip of stiffening 1½ or 2 inches wide and long enough to cover top of skirt. Cut a strip of fabric twice this width plus ½ inch all around for seams. Cut any interlining same size as fabric and baste it to wrong side of fabric. Place stiffening on wrong side at lower edge of fabric, ½ inch from edges. Fold the ½ inch of fabric over it and baste (Fig. 306 a). Baste remaining seam allowance of fabric to wrong side. Place stiffened half of band against right side of skirt and fold free half of band over the top to wrong side (Fig. 306 b). Sew edges in place by hand or topstitch.

Shaped Band (see Fig. 304): Cut a strip of stiffening desired width for shaping lower edge, long enough to cover top of skirt. Cut a strip of fabric twice this width, plus ½-inch seam allowance on all sides. Place stiffening on wrong side of fabric, ½ inch from lower edge. Draw outline of shaping on a piece of paper and place this over lower edge of stiffening. Pin, then baste together and stitch on outline. Tear away paper. Trim off seam allowance ½ inch from stitching line, then trim off excess stiffening close to stitching line. Clip into seam allowance at corners and around any curves of shaping. Turn right side out and press. Turn under seam allowance on remainder of fabric and fold band in half over top of skirt. Sew in place.

215

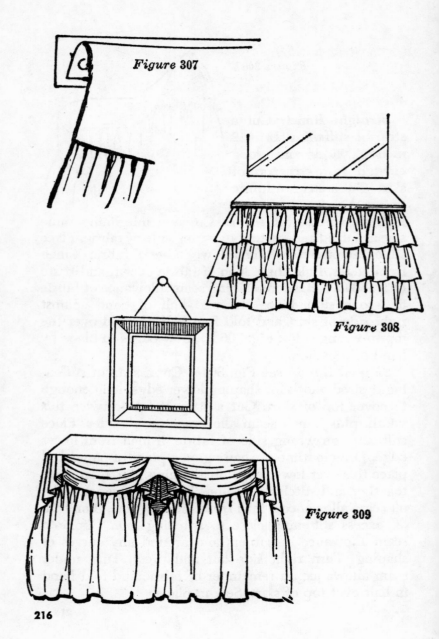

Figure 307

Figure 308

Figure 309

To Attach Skirt: There are several ways to do this.

1. Sew a tape under the band, leaving lower edge of tape free. Tack skirt to dressing table through this tape, underneath the skirt (Fig. 307).

2. Sew one-half of snap tape to wrong side of band. Tack other half of tape to edge of table, making sure that snaps will meet.

3. If there is a mirror or glass top, cut a piece of fabric to fit under the glass, allowing ½-inch seam allowance. Sew skirt to this piece, making a slip-cover for the table.

4. Trim the band with gimp, then tack to edge of table with gimp tacks.

Ruffled Skirt: Make and attach ruffles as for ruffled curtains on page 142 (Fig. 308).

Swags: (Fig. 309). The method for making these is

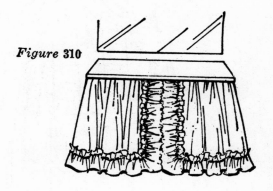

Figure 310

given on page 163. They should be basted in place on skirt before the band is added.

Flounced Skirt: Make a plain skirt with slight fullness, then sew on the flounces, overlapping them about 1 inch. Finish top with band (Fig. 310).

Overskirt: (Fig. 311). Make two skirts, with top skirt in two sections. Join them at the top and attach band. Drape overskirt to the sides and fasten with rosettes, tassels or other ornaments.

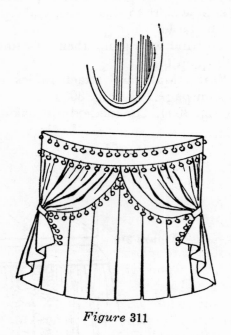

Figure 311

Refinishing Furniture

NEVER DISCARD any good furniture until you have imagined it in a new setting with the various transformations that can be made. Cheap furniture is seldom worth the time and trouble involved, but fine pieces of honest wood cost money and will usually last for several lifetimes if given the proper care and reconditioning treatment. An old-fashioned dressing table might be waxed, stained or painted to make a handsome desk; that battered table could be provided with a skirt and mirrored top to serve as a dressing table. Perhaps a buffet can have the legs cut down and be transformed into a hi-fi unit; those dining room chairs you no longer need—how about gilding them and tying on tasseled velvet cushions, to turn them into occasional chairs for an entry or bedroom?

Before planning a reupholstery job, examine the bottom rails. Test the wood with a sharp knife to determine whether it is hardwood or softwood. Hardwood can stand up for many years and is worth redoing. Pine, used in cheap furniture, is too soft for holding tacks properly. Very old chairs that have been recovered many times, may be riddled with tack holes, but unless the wood has splintered, these can be filled with plastic wood.

CLEANING AND REFINISHING WOOD

This is the time, before the upholstery is put on a piece of furniture, to clean it thoroughly, "strip" it or restore oils, waxes and polishes to it. It depends on the amount of restoring and renovating needed.

When you have taken off all the old upholstery, taken out the springs, reduced the piece to the bare frame, you are then able to evaluate what needs to be done. If the frame seems shaky you can strengthen it at the joints by using angle irons or mending plates of light metal, which are obtainable in any hardware store, at variety stores, even at the five-and-dimes.

If only cleaning of the wood is indicated the process is very simple; if the piece is "oil-starved," again the process is easy. If complete "stripping" of all finish is needed the steps take longer. You will require a good liquid remover that takes off paint, lacquer, enamel, varnish or shellac. We give you the procedure for doing this at the end of this section.

To restore any piece in fairly good condition you may need only to use the following. Fill any cracks with a wood-filler obtainable in a paint shop, choosing a color to match that of the wood you are working on. When this is dry a gentle sanding with fine sandpaper will bevel the "fill" down so it is not noticeable. Next, use a wax paste, the color of your piece. There are two types on the market—one for light woods, such as pine, maple, light cherry; one for dark woods, such as mahogany, rosewood, all the brown or reddish-brown woods.

You will also find in department stores, in hardware

and paint shops, two kinds of "scratch sticks"—one for dark woods, one for blond woods. These cost about a dollar. When drawn across a scratch they obliterate the scratch mark and restore the original color. They do not, however, obliterate the scratch itself. They simply blend the color so the scratch is not noticeable.

Pine and Maple Furniture: If there is an accumulation of soil, wash the piece with a mild white soap and lukewarm water. Do *not* use a detergent. Use old face cloths or pieces of turkish toweling well wrung out. Rinse off traces of soap with cloths dipped in clear water. When the wood is thoroughly dry use a very fine pumice powder (# f.f.f.) moistened in crude oil; rub this into the wood with an old bath towel or soft cheesecloth. Wipe off. Remove all traces of oil and finally buff with a good quality of light-colored paste wax.

Mahogany and Dark Woods: To remove soil, use mild white soap—never a detergent—but do *not* use on any deep carvings. These should be done later when the piece is dry by using finely powdered pumice stone and crude oil applied with a toothbrush. When using oil with the pumice stone powder pour the oil slowly, drop by drop, as you clean into the carvings. After using benzine on a soft cloth to remove all traces of pumice stone and grit, the final step is waxing. First allow the piece to dry for 24 hours. Then apply wax very lightly so that no lumps or thicknesses of wax result, making the surface bumpy or uneven. Two thin coats are much better than one heavy coat. Use a dark wax. If you can find them in your locality, there are some wonderful "satin" waxes made by an English firm and long used by professional furniture restorers.

These waxes come in lemon-verbena, lavender, and rose scent. The odor of furniture polished with these waxes is indeed lovely. A fine patina is obtained by buffing after waxing, either by hand or by an electric sander with polisher attachment (these may be rented in most localities). For those sufficiently fortunate to own an electric hand-sander and polisher, a high, durable gloss can be given furniture in almost the proverbial shake of a lambswool tail!

Removing Wood Finish: To remove all the finish right down to the base wood you may wish to use a reputable brand of paint and varnish remover. There are some excellent ones on the market obtainable at hardware and paint stores. Never attempt to hand-scrape the old surfaces as you are apt to gouge the wood; and if you have a really valuable antique that needs a complete refinishing, it is economy in the long run to send it out to an expert cabinetmaker or refinisher. But for the average "re-do" the home craftsman can achieve notable results.

When "stripping" with solvent work out of doors if possible. If this is not feasible, clear as large a work space as you can manage in a basement or a room where there is adequate ventilation.

A paint remover of the "wash-away" variety is the easiest to use. Flow the remover on with a small paint brush, being careful to brush in one direction only. Do not brush *across* a previous stroke or across the grain. The finish will soften in five to thirty minutes, depending on how many layers of old finish or paint have accumulated. Follow the instructions on your paint-remover container as chemical contents vary in different products. When the finish is properly softened, test it with a fingertip. If a heavy "sludge" has loosened you may use cardboard pieces to sluff it off, bit by bit. If you are using a "wash-away" remover, wash off the remaining "sludge" with very wet rags and cool water. Keep rinsing the rags that take up the "sludge." To get into deep carvings use an old toothbrush or nail brush. When the finish piles up on the brush, simply rinse it well or hold it under a running-water tap.

SCREWS TO USE IN REPAIRING CHAIRS

One of the construction points to inspect when re-doing old chairs is the *corner block* at each joint of the frame. Turn your chair upside down and test the strength of these corner blocks; if the screws have worked loose, remove them. If the screws are bent, worn or obviously now too small for the holes because of wearing away or "flaking" of the wood, purchase new ones. Use the removed screws for comparison when buying new screws. Measure them. The following is a chart of the most commonly used lengths:

$$
\begin{array}{rcl}
\text{No.} & 4 & = \tfrac{1}{2} \text{ inch} \\
\text{No.} & 5 & = \tfrac{5}{8} \text{ inch} \\
\text{No.} & 6 & = \tfrac{3}{4} \text{ inch} \\
\text{No.} & 7 & = 1 \text{ inch} \\
\text{No.} & 8 & = 1\tfrac{1}{4} \text{ inch} \\
\text{No.} & 10 & = 1\tfrac{1}{2} \text{ inch} \\
\text{No.} & 11 & = 1\tfrac{3}{4} \text{ inch} \\
\text{No.} & 12 & = 2 \text{ inch}
\end{array}
$$

Reupholstering Furniture

IT IS TRULY surprising how much fun it can be to upholster a piece of furniture. Do not be afraid to tackle your first job, but start with a straight chair, a stool or a bench, because this is a learn-as-you-go process. The techniques you acquire on a small piece will provide the skill and confidence that you will need to take on more ambitious projects.

Here is a list of the tools and equipment you will need:

Webbing-Stretcher (Fig. 312): This is essential to hold the webbing tight across the frame when tacking it in place. The end of the stretcher opposite the prongs

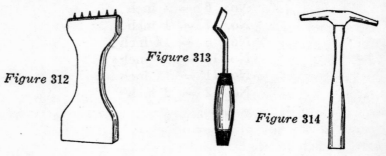

Figure 312

Figure 313

Figure 314

Figure 315

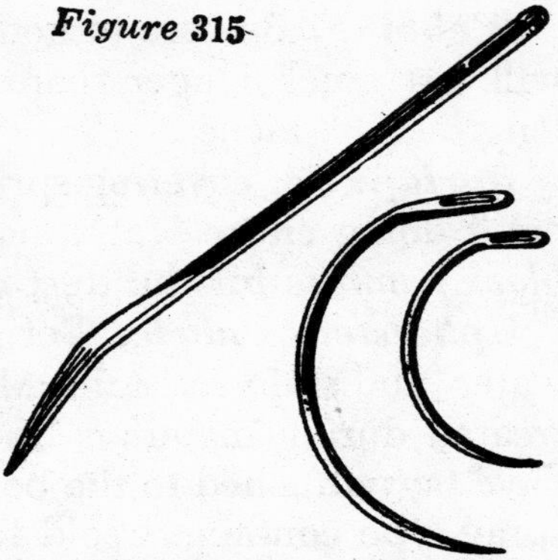

should be padded to
keep it from marring the
furniture.

Tack Remover (Fig.
313): Sharper than most
claw-hammers, this will
help pry up the tacks
more easily.

Tack Hammer (Fig. 314): The magnetized head
will hold the tack and drive it in place with one opera-
tion. A small hammer may be substituted, but too large
a hammer is awkward to wield in corners or small
spaces.

Heavy-Duty Scissors: For cutting burlap, webbing
and twine.

Spring Twine: A heavy twine for tying the springs.

Stitching Twine: A fine, firm twine or *carpet thread,*
for sewing springs to burlap and sewing padded rolls
of burlap in place.

Upholstery Needles (Fig. 315): These include
curved needles, a long needle with curved point and a
very long needle to penetrate several thicknesses of
padding.

Upholsterers' Tacks: These come in a variety of
sizes from tiny ones to nearly 1 inch in length for different uses. The sizes you will need for most upholstery
are 4-oz., 6-oz., 8-oz. and 12-oz. As you remove tacks
from dust cover, webbing, burlap and muslin, take
note of the various sizes and use similar sizes for the
same steps. Be sure that tacks have flat heads. If using
many thicknesses, you may need the longest tacks (20-
oz.), which are slightly under 1 inch.

Webbing: Be sure to get good jute webbing, which will last much longer than a cheap grade. The usual length is 3½ inches.

Burlap: For covering springs (enough for three layers if doing entire seat), *muslin* to cover padding and *black cambric* for the dust cover.

Upholstery Fabric: Get a good quality, preferably water- and stain-resistant. Many fine fabrics have been treated during manufacture to eliminate spotting and have tags attached to the bolts to verify the claim. The spray-type containers sold for water-proofing may not make the fabric soil-resistant. Be sure to read the label carefully before buying or using them.

Gimp: This is the narrow braid used to cover the raw edges of upholstery fabric where it is attached to the wooden frame. If gimp is used, you will need *upholsterers' glue for fabrics* or *gimp tacks,* which have small round heads. The lengths vary from 5/16 to 10/16 inch.

Decorative Upholstery Nails (Fig. 316): These

Figure 316

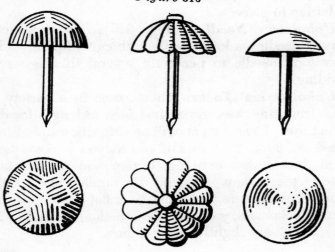

may be used instead of gimp to cover the edges of fabric with a row of nail heads close together.

Figure 317

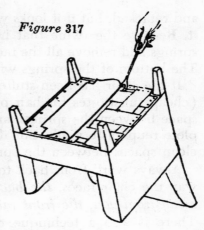

Stuffing: The best stuffing is horsehair, which can be fluffed and reused. Other stuffing includes moss, foam rubber cushioning and Acrilan. Use plenty of stuffing, because it should be firm and packed down when covered.

Padding: Sheet wadding or slab foam rubber will be used as a final layer over the basic stuffing.

Plastic Wood: Useful for refilling old tack holes so that new tacks will hold firmly.

REPAIRING BOTTOM OF CHAIR

The most common repair necessary to chairs and sofas is retying the springs and replacing or retacking the webbing that sags below the bottom of the chair. If the top of the seat is even and still firm, proceed as follows:

Turn the chair upside down at a convenient height on a sturdy table. Remove the cambric dust cover (Fig. 317) and pull out all the tacks holding it. Examine the webbing. If it is in good condition and has merely pulled away from the rails, it can be stretched and retacked, but if it looks worn or dried out, replace it. Remove the twine that holds the webbing to the springs and remove all the tacks from the bottom rails. The bottom of the springs will now be exposed.

If the chair has been stuffed with excelsior or straw (cheap substitutes for hair or moss), this will fill the space between the springs, and you should do a complete reupholstery job. But if the top looks firm, with clean spaces between the springs, retie the springs.

Always work from back to front. No matter which way the chair faces, *the back rail is the one farthest away from you, the front rail is the one nearest you.* There is also a technique called *baste-tacking;* this means to drive a tack part way into the rail.

The springs are set in even rows and must be tied to hold them firmly from back to front and from side to side. Starting at the back rail about ¾ inch from outer edge, baste-tack two tacks in line with each row of springs. Cut a piece of spring twine about 1 yard long. Make a slip-knot in one end of the twine and loop the knot securely around one of the two tacks, then drive this tack home. Loop the twine around the second tack and drive in this tack. Check to make sure the tacks will hold the twine tight; if necessary, drive another tack into the twine between the first two tacks.

Loop the twine over the far side of the back spring, then over the near side of the same spring. Continue in this way to front rail, looping the twine twice over each spring. Baste-tack two tacks in the front rail in line with the spring. Now adjust the twine so that all the springs are even and no higher than the rails, pulling the twine tight. When it is taut and evenly spaced, loop it around one of the front tacks and drive the tack home; loop it around the other tack and drive in this tack. Check to make sure twine is secure, tacking it again if necessary. Cut off excess twine. Tie the other rows of springs in the same way, keeping them all the same height. Now turn the chair around or stand at the side and tie the springs across, this time knotting the twine around the far side of the spring, around the other twine at center of spring and around the near side of spring, across each row (Fig. 318). Two more tyings, this time diagonally across, will keep the springs tight and firm (Fig. 319); each spring will be tied in eight places, and the twine will be knotted together at the center of springs.

Next comes the webbing. Start the first strip at center of back rail. Hold it against the rail with the raw end at *inner* edge of rail, then tack it with three tacks about ½ inch from outer edge of rail (Fig. 320). Fold the webbing down toward you, over these tacks, making sure that fold is ½ inch from outer rail to allow room for attaching dust cover, and secure with two more tacks placed between the first three tacks (Fig. 321).

Bring the webbing straight across to the front rail and insert the prongs of the webbing-stretcher up through the webbing about 3 inches beyond the rail (Fig. 322). Brace the padded end against the side of the rail and *pull*. When the webbing is as tight as you can get it, drive in three tacks—this is where the tack hammer can be of help; it can be used with one hand while you hold the webbing-stretcher with the other. Without the tack hammer, you will need someone to

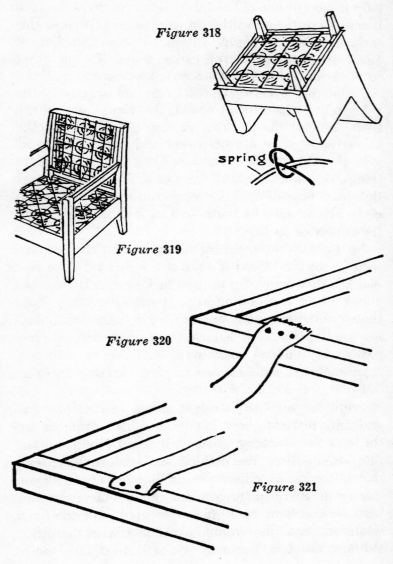

Figure 318

spring

Figure 319

Figure 320

Figure 321

lend an extra hand. Fold the end of the webbing over the three tacks and drive in two more tacks as before. Cut off excess webbing.

Space webbing evenly across the entire chair seat from back to front, having the rows close together; if the rails are curved, try the webbing across the chair before tacking to see at what angle it should be folded to fit the curve (Fig. 323).

Turn the chair around and attach webbing to back rail, then weave it over and under the first strips to the front rail (Fig. 324). Using the webbing-stretcher, attach this strip with three tacks, fold over end and drive in two tacks, cut webbing. Weave remaining strips across in this direction in the same way. Webbing must now be sewed to the springs to keep the springs in position. For this, use the sewing twine or carpet thread and the needle with the curved tip. Sew each spring to webbing in three or four places, carrying the twine across one row of springs, then back across the next row. Knot each end of twine securely when starting and fastening off.

Allowing 1 inch all around, cut cambric to fit the bottom of the chair, covering the rails to within ¼ inch of outer edges. Turn under edge and tack to back rail, using small tacks about 1 inch apart, pull taut and tack to front rail, turning under raw edge. Where cambric fits around legs, mark the line with chalk where it meets the wood, clip the edges beyond the chalk line (see Fig. 99 on page 80), turn under the raw edges and tack. When back and front have been securely fastened, turn chair around and tack in same way from back to front.

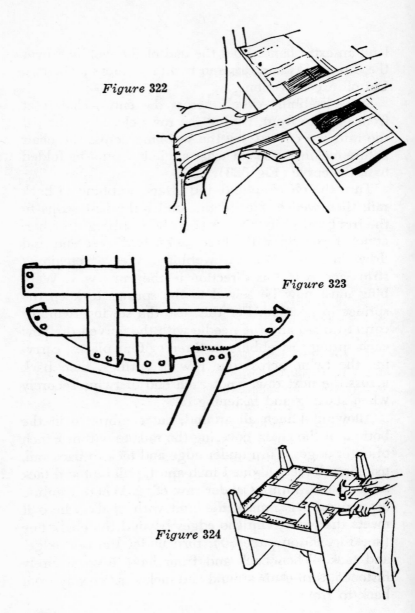

Figure 322

Figure 323

Figure 324

REUPHOLSTERING THE ENTIRE SEAT OF A STRAIGHT CHAIR

Turn the chair upside down on a table, remove the dust cover and webbing. Cut off the twine that holds springs to webbing. Pull out all the tacks as you go, noting the different sizes by taping a tack to a piece of paper and jotting down whether it was used for holding dust cover, webbing, burlap, spring twine, etc.

Turn the chair right side up and remove the gimp or upholsterers' nails, the top cover and muslin, padding and stuffing, burlap, webbing and springs. Pull out all the tacks.

If the legs are weak, brace them with wood blocks screwed to legs and rails where they join, or reinforce them with angle irons. They may only need reglueing; if so, scrape off as much of the old glue as you can reach, fill the crevice with glue and tie the joint firmly until the glue sets and dries. Old tack holes can be filled with plastic wood—allow this to dry thoroughly before you start work. Rails that have splintered can be replaced by a cabinetmaker if the rest of the chair is in good enough condition to warrant the cost. This is also the time to refinish the wood while there is no upholstery to worry about. A missing bit of wood, broken off the corner of a leg or on a carved back, can be replaced or rebuilt. Drive a couple of tacks into the broken surface, letting the heads protrude to form an anchor for the plastic wood, which is then built up around them and over them until it fills the contour. When this has set, it can be sanded into the proper shape, then stained and waxed to match the rest of the frame.

When the bare frame has been restored to good condition, start by fastening the webbing across the bottom rails as described for repairing the bottom of a chair. Turn the chair right side up and stand the springs on the webbing to see how they should be spaced. The top of the spring is where the tip is turned down

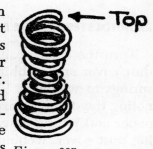

Figure 325

(Fig. 325). This curved tip should always be facing the center of the chair. Mark the position of the springs on the webbing with a pencil. Remove all but one spring. Holding this spring in place, sew the bottom coil to the webbing with stitching twine or carpet thread. Use the curved needle or the needle with the curved tip and work from the bottom of the chair, checking the position of the spring frequently. Sew the other springs to the webbing, one at a time. Tie the tops of the springs to the top rails in the same way as for repairing the bottom of a chair seat, holding down springs so that they are about 3 inches higher than the rails; the center springs should be slightly higher to form the "crown" of the seat. Manipulate each spring as it is tied to keep it straight.

Next, cut a piece of burlap, leaving a margin that will extend about 6 inches beyond the rails on all four sides. Using tacks with heads that are large enough to hold the burlap in place, tack across back rail with tacks about 1 inch apart and about ½ inch from outer edge of rail. Tack on the other three sides—do not pull the burlap too tight, but keep it smooth across the springs. Using stitching twine or carpet thread and curved needle, sew the burlap to the springs, catching each spring in three or four places.

Cut diagonally into each corner of the burlap margin. Turn this margin toward center, enclosing a 2-inch roll of stuffing (Fig. 326) and tucking in the raw edge under the roll. Sew the inner edge of the roll to the burlap cover—this roll will cushion the edges of the seat by covering the rails. When making the next roll, enclose the corner from the previous roll; if this cannot be done because of intervening posts, tuck the corners inside the roll.

Fill the center with stuffing or a foam-rubber cushion cut and beveled to fit. Use plenty of stuffing—almost twice the amount you would expect to fill the seat properly. Do not skimp, or the chair will be too soft and the seat too low. The final covers will hold the stuffing down. Make sure that you cannot feel the springs through the stuffing. Throw a piece of muslin over the stuffing and sit on the chair to see how it

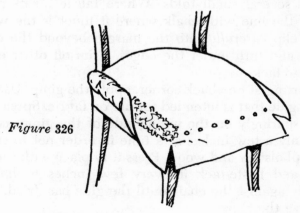

Figure 326

feels. Smooth the stuffing evenly and cover it with burlap or muslin, sewing the edges to the rolls around the
sides. Then add a layer of cotton padding or a slab of
foam rubber to cover the entire seat smoothly. If using
foam rubber, taper the sides to avoid square edges.

Next comes the muslin cover. Tack this firmly around
all four sides, stretching it taut so it holds the stuffing
and padding evenly rounded. Over the muslin goes the
upholstery fabric. Place it on the chair before any cutting is done. The straight of the goods must run from
back to front with any pattern centered. Pile fabric,
such as velvet, plush, velveteen or corduroy, should
brush toward the front of the chair.

If you plan to use gimp, determine where the gimp
will go; it must cover both the raw edges of the fabric
and the tacks that hold the fabric in place, so the tacks
must be put close to edges of the upholstery material.
Baste-tack the fabric in place until it is even, then
cut away excess; check position of tacks and drive
them in. At rounded corners ease in the fullness or
make several small folds. Where fabric meets posts,
mark the line with chalk where it touches the wood,
then clip *carefully* into the margin beyond the chalk
mark and turn under the edges. Trim off other edges
close to tacks.

Starting at one back corner, apply the gimp. Use any
good glue that is intended for use on fabric. Spread the
glue sparingly on the wrong side of the gimp, covering only a few inches at a time in order not to smear
the upholstery and wood. Press it in place with the fin-
gers and baste-tack it every few inches to hold it
tightly against the chair until the glue has dried, then
remove the tacks.

If you plan to use decorative nails, the edge of the fabric must be turned under all around, so allow for this when cutting. Turn under ½ inch and baste-tack, keeping the folded edge straight. Cut a strip of cardboard as a guide for placing nails. Mark one straight long edge with a pencil, spacing the marks evenly; if you want the nailheads touching, space the marks the width of the nailheads; otherwise, use a ruler to space the marks about ½ inch apart. Hold the cardboard just above the edge of the fold and baste-tack a nail at each mark. Move the cardboard, drive in all but the last nail, replace cardboard under the last nail and continue around in this way.

It is also possible to attach gimp with gimp tacks, al-though this does not prove as effective as gluing. Start at one back corner and tack the gimp in place, covering the raw edge of upholstery and the upholstery tacks. The gimp should follow the folded edges around the posts where it cannot be tacked. If it fits snugly, let it be. If it seems loose, catch it in place with the small curved needle and sewing thread.

Last, put on the dust cover, then stand back and admire your handiwork.

REUPHOLSTERING ARMCHAIRS AND OVERSTUFFED FURNITURE

These are major jobs—do not attempt them unless you have done several smaller pieces successfully and feel adventurous enough to tackle an extensive project. It takes time, patience and careful workmanship. A valuable piece is worth all this effort; a cheap piece might be worth recovering to gain experience.

Here are additional rules to guide you.

The last pieces put on are the first to come off, these include the dust cover, the outside back, then the outside arms and the front border. Remove them carefully to use as patterns and take note of how they were attached and where welting was used. Keep track of the tack sizes. You will see that the inside back, arms and platform covers are drawn through to the outside rails where they are attached.

If the stuffing, webbing and springs are in good condition, leave them alone; but if they are sagging you will have to strip them and rebuild them, preferably one section at a time—if the entire chair is stripped, you may have trouble replacing the springs in their correct positions. Figs. 327, 328, 329 and 330 show the basic construction, layer by layer, of one typical chair. While you are about it, use new webbing and burlap to replace the old, thus insuring a longer life to the piece, and either replace or add to the stuffing for a firmer shape. After each section has been

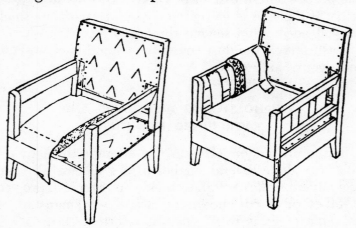

Figure 327   *Figure 328*

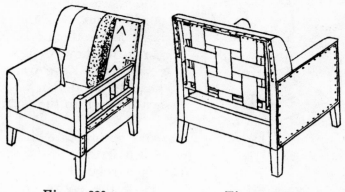

Figure 329   *Figure* 330

rebuilt, cut the new upholstery fabric, using the old pieces as patterns. Allow about 2 inches all around each section to fit over the added fullness and for working margins.

In the directions for slipcovers you will find Fig. 44, which shows the straight of goods on each piece. Pile fabric should brush forward on the seat and down toward the floor on the other sections. Be sure to center patterns. See pages 47–51 for making welting.

Following the seam lines on the old cover, sew the inside arms and inside back together; these seams may have been welted, so follow the original method. On some chairs these seams may not be necessary because each piece is covered separately. Tack these pieces in place on the frame, keeping fabric straight and evenly taut, and easing in or pleating the fabric on curved edges. Cover the seat. The other pieces must now be put on in the same order as before, each piece covering the raw edges of another section.

The outside arms probably go on next to cover the

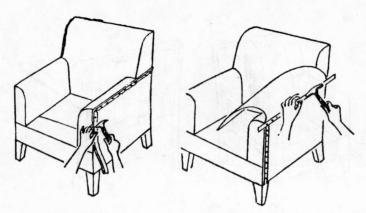

raw edges of the inside arms. Tack on the welting (Fig. 331); if it also covers front border, welt the side edge, too. Now cut a 2-inch strip of cardboard to hold the welted edge firm. Position the top edge of fabric on arm. Turn up the fabric, exposing the raw edge underneath. Cover this raw edge with the strip of cardboard (Fig. 332) and tack in place with the tacks about ½ inch apart. Turn down the fabric and tack lower edge under bottom rail; tack back edge to back of frame. Welt and tack the top edge of front border with a strip of cardboard in the same way.

If there are front arm panels, welt these on side and top edges. Since these cannot be tacked all around from underneath, cut cardboard to fit the welted edges, with both panels exactly the same. Turn the raw edges of fabric over the cardboard and baste-tack in place. Using the curved needle and carpet thread, sew in place on the inner side of welting so that the stitches will lie hidden between welting and fabric (Fig. 333).

Side back panels are applied in the same way, *except*

that the side edges are usually covered by the outside back and need not be welted. Last of all, welt the outside back (Fig. 334). Tack fabric to chair, using cardboard stripping across the top, unless this is curved; join a curved back in the same way as front arm panels.

Tack all the lower edges under the bottom rails, then attach the dust cover (Fig. 335). If you wish to add a skirt, make the skirt in the same way as for a slipcover. Pin it in place to see how it fits and to check that the finished length and depth fit chair exactly. Mark and stitch the top edge, securing any pleats in place. Tack welting to chair, then tack skirt over welting and strips of cardboard in the same way as outside arms. The lower edge of chair can also be finished with fringe or gimp; use glue or gimp tacks to attach the trimming.

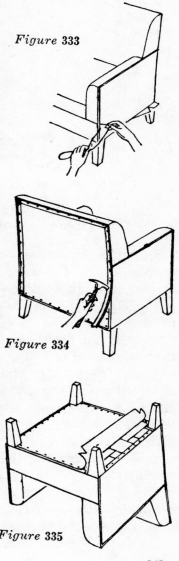

Figure 333

Figure 334

Figure 335

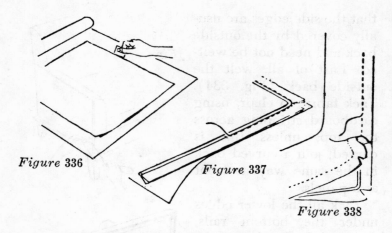

Figure 336

Figure 337

Figure 338

RECOVERING CHAIR CUSHIONS

Spring cushions are very apt to sag and become uncomfortable. Instead of replacing or repairing the springs, take the cushion cover to your local foam-rubber dealer and buy or order a foam-rubber cushion to fit.

Rip the old cover carefully and notch the corners, then cut a new one (Fig. 336). Welt top and bottom sections (Fig. 337). Matching notches, sew border to top section (Fig. 338). Leaving an opening large enough to insert cushion at back of cover, sew border to bottom section. Insert cushion and pin opening together. Using curved needle and carpet thread, sew edges of opening together, hiding the stitches under welting.

Special Threads: There are also other types of thread for special purposes:

Synthetic Thread: An extra strong thread of textured

THREAD AND NEEDLE CHART*

	FABRIC	THREAD	SEWING NEEDLE	MACHINE NEEDLE
VERY SHEER	marquisette, net, ninon, chiffon	colors: Mercerized Sewing thread in 170 colors (use thread one shade darker than fabric); black: size 70; white; sizes 100, 120 150	size 10	finest size 16 stitches per inch
SHEER	dotted swiss, organdy, voile, sheer crepe	colors: Mercerized Sewing thread in 170 colors (use thread one shade darker than fabric); black or white: size 70	size 9	fine size 16 stitches per inch
MEDIUM LIGHT WEIGHT	gingham, percale, challis, taffeta, sheer wool crepe, satin, surah	colors: Mercerized Sewing thread in 170 colors (use thread one shade darker than fabric); black or white: size 60 or 70	sizes 8, 9	fine size 12 stitches per inch
MEDIUM	flannel, shantung, chintz, seersucker, sateen, velveteen, pique, broadcloth, corduroy, linen, faille, jersey.	colors: Mercerized Sewing thread in 170 colors (use thread one shade darker than fabric); black or white: size 50 or 60	sizes 7, 8	medium size 12 stitches per inch
MEDIUM HEAVY WEIGHT	terrycloth, burlap, quilted fabric, drapery fabric, denim, suiting, tweed, gabardine, coating, felt, fleece	colors: Heavy-Duty Mercerized Sewing thread in 60 colors plus black and white; or black, white: size 36, 40	size 6	medium coarse size 10 stitches per inch
HEAVY	sailcloth, upholstery fabric, ticking	colors: Heavy-Duty Mercerized Sewing thread in 60 colors plus black and white; or black, white: size 24, 30, 36	sizes 4, 5	coarse size 8 stitches per inch
VERY HEAVY	awning cloth, canvas, duck	black or white: size 8, 10, 20	sizes 1, 2, 3	coarsest size 6 stitches per inch

* Courtesy of Coats & Clark's "O.N.T." Threads and Milwards Needles

nylon, which is strong enough for any weight fabric, has the feel of cotton and comes in black, white and twenty-eight colors. Do *not* use on untreated cotton or linen. Excellent for wash-and-wear.

Button and Carpet Thread: An extra strong, heavily glazed cotton thread for hand sewing only. Good for upholstery, comes in eight colors plus black and white.

Quilting Thread: A fine, strong, heavily glazed cotton thread for hand or machine quilting. Available in thirteen colors plus white (no black).

Dressmaker Spool Mercerized Sewing Thread: In black or white, sizes 40, 50 and 60. These jumbo spools are a time-saver for machine sewing.

Special Needles: There are hand-sewing and machine-sewing needles of many different sizes. High quality needles that will not cut or fray the thread will facilitate the sewing on slipcovers, curtains and upholstery. Select needles in the length that is comfortable to use for each purpose. "Sharps" have a round eye, "crewel" needles have a long eye, which some people find easier to thread. Packaged needles range in assorted sizes from 3 to 9 and from 5 to 10. Various brands of sewing machines have different size-mark-

ZIPPER CHART*

USE FOR	ZIPPER TYPES	COLORS	LENGTHS
One-Piece Slipcovers	Slipcover Zippers	Tan Only	24", 27", 30", 36"
Sectional Slipcovers	Heavy Jacket	Beige, Brown, Gray, Black	14", 16", 18", 20", 22"
	Light Jacket	14 colors	10", 12", 14", 16" 18", 20"
Pillow Sham	Dress Placket	37 colors	9", 10", 12", 14"

*Courtesy of Coats & Clark Inc.

ings, so ask for fine, medium or coarse. There are also *quilting needles, upholsterers' needles* and even beading needles.

Use this Chart to Approximate Yardage Requirements for Plain Fabrics*
(Patterned Fabrics require more yardage as indicated)

Furniture Type	Cushions	Material 48″ wide		Material 30″ wide		Welting or Trimming
		Plain Material	Figured or Striped	Plain Material	Figured or Striped	
Sofa	3	14 yds.	15½ yds.	21 yds.	23 yds.	36 yds.
	1 loose	13½ yds.	15 yds.	20½ yds.	22½ yds.	33 yds.
	none	10 yds.	11 yds.	15 yds.	17 yds.	21 yds.
Love Seat	2	10 yds.	11 yds.	15 yds.	16½ yds.	24 yds.
	1	10 yds.	11 yds.	15 yds.	16½ yds.	23 yds.
	none	8½ yds.	9¼ yds.	12¾ yds.	14¼ yds.	14 yds.
Arm Chair	1	7½ yds.	8¼ yds.	11¼ yds.	12¼ yds.	18 yds.
	none	6 yds.	6¾ yds.	8⅓ yds.	9½ yds.	13 yds.
Boudoir Chair	1	5 yds.	5¾ yds.	7¾ yds.	8¾ yds.	15 yds.
	none	4½ yds.	5¼ yds.	7½ yds.	7½ yds.	12 yds.
Wing Chair	1	8 yds.	9 yds.	12 yds.	13½ yds.	18 yds.
	none	6½ yds.	7¼ yds.	9¾ yds.	10¾ yds.	13 yds.
Cogswell Chair	1	7 yds.	8 yds.	10½ yds.	12 yds.	16 yds.
	none	5½ yds.	6 yds.	8¼ yds.	9 yds.	11 yds.
Daybed and Mattress	3	14½ yds.	16 yds.	21¾ yds.	23¾ yds.	42 yds.
	none	11 yds.	12 yds.	17 yds.	19½ yds.	27 yds.
Daybed	3	11 yds.	12 yds.	16½ yds.	18 yds.	29 yds.
	none	7½ yds.	8¼ yds.	11 yds.	12¼ yds.	14 yds.
Ottoman	none	2 yds.	2½ yds.	3 yds.	3½ yds.	6 yds.
Chaise Lounge	1	10 yds.	11 yds.	15 yds.	16½ yds.	23 yds.
	none	8 yds.	9 yds.	12 yds.	13¼ yds.	16 yds.
Dining Room Chair	none	1½ yds.	1¾ yds.	1⅚ yds.	2⅙ yds	5½ yds.
Extra Cushion	1	1¼ yds.	1¾ yds.	1⅚ yds.	2⅙ yds.	5 yds.

*Courtesy of Consolidated Trimming Corp.

ABOUT THE AUTHORS

Marguerite Maddox, through her syndicated newspaper columns and wide contacts in every section of the United States over a period of many years, intimately knows the needs of the home decorator and needlewoman.

Miriam Morrison Peake, magazine editor, author and consultant, has specialized in searching out the problems that plague the amateur and finding ways to simplify instructions.

Index

251

Roman, 171-73
Window treatments, 86-95
Windows, kinds of, 89-92
Wing chairs, 67-68
Wood:
    hard, 219
    "oil-starved," 220
    pine, 219
    plastic, 219
    soft, 219
Wood, cleaning and refinishing,
    220-23
    hand scraping, 222
    mahogany and dark woods,
    221-22
    maple furniture, 221
    paint remover, 220, 222-23
    pine furniture, 221
    pumice powder, 221
    removing wood finish, 222-23

"scratch sticks," 221
stripping, 220
wax, paste, 220-21
waxing, 220, 221-22
wood-filler, 220
Wood-filler, 220
Wooden bolsters, to cover, 202,
    205-6

Y

Yardage, measuring:
    bedspreads, two-piece, 191-92
    curtain, 111-17
Yardstick, 29

Z

Zippers, 27-28, 51, 53
    bed pillow covers, 207, 208,
    209
    chart, 244
    insertion in slipcover, 61